SHIVA

SHUBHA VILAS

FiNGERPRINT!

Published by

FiNGERPRINT!

An imprint of Prakash Books India Pvt. Ltd.

113/A, Darya Ganj,
New Delhi-110 002
Email: info@prakashbooks.com/sales@prakashbooks.com

facebook www.facebook.com/fingerprintpublishing
twitter www.twitter.com/FingerprintP
www.fingerprintpublishing.com

ISBN: 978 93 5440 898 4

Processed & printed in India

Author's note

Lord Shiva is one of the most adored, venerated, and worshipped personalities in the Vedas. Yet understanding him completely is almost impossible. He has such a unique personality that all paradoxes rest in him simultaneously and dynamically. This book is my little humble attempt to place my head at the feet of Lord Shiva and allow his grace to flow in the form of stories that the reader can relish, absorb, and celebrate. I do not claim to be a scholar or an authority on a subject as great as Lord Shiva, but I consider myself a modest student trying to dive into the oceanic depths of the Shiva tattva and bring out some beautiful gems to absorb into our minds.

There are four main tattvas in the Vedic culture. The Vishnu tattva, Shakti tattva, Shambhu tattva, and Jiva tattva. The word tattva means principle, reality, or energy. These four are the principal energies predominating the universe. All incarnations of Lord Vishnu fall within the ambit of the Vishnu Tattva. The Shakti tattva consists of all manifestations of energy in the form of Sita, Radha, Durga, Lakshmi, etc. The divine feminine energy that pervades the universe and intercedes in every aspect of governance is ordained as the Shakti Tattva. The Jiva tattva is manifest in all forms of living beings that have a material body, including the devatas, gandharvas, apsaras, humans, animals, birds, plants, etc. Any soul that is engulfed in a subtle or gross bodily covering falls under the Jiva tattva category, which extends all the way from a plant to Lord Brahma. This brings us to the most interesting of the four tattvas, which is the Shambhu tattva. He is so unique in position that the entire tattva consists of just one person, and that is Lord Shiva. This book is a dedication to that enigmatic deity that is etched in the hearts of millions.

The position of Lord Shiva is very beautifully explained in the Brahma Samhita (Verse 45): "When milk is transformed into curd with the addition of acids, curd is neither the same nor very different from milk. I worship the primeval Lord Govinda, who transforms into the state of Shambhu to take up the task of destruction."

This book explores many interesting features of Lord Shiva through surreal stories. How did Kubera take up residence near Kailash? What happened when Narada Muni offered a single mango to Ganesha and Kartikeya? And many more stories revolving around Ravana, Daksha, Nandi, Kings, and demons will charm every heart and deepen your love for Lord Shiva. As Bhubaneshwar, Gangadhar, Mallikarjuna, Nandieshwar, and Gopeshwar, his divine *lilas* instilled faith and devotion.

The stories explore various facets of Lord Shiva. Shiva is called Ashutosh, the one who is easily satisfied. His kind heart wants to accommodate everyone and offer benedictions to both the good and the bad, with the hope that someday the bad will transform into the good through the power of his association. His associates are ghosts and hobgoblins who are rejected by society. He welcomes them and accepts them as his own family without any discrimination. He embraces everyone with their faults and thus paves a roadway deep into their hearts. Once he is established in your heart, he gently instills faith and devotion to the Lord. Shiva is known as Vishwas Murti, or the deity of faith. His faith in the Supreme Lord is unparalleled, and it manifests so powerfully when he appears as Hanuman to serve Lord Rama.

The sacrifices that Lord Shiva makes for universal well-being endear him even further. When Halahal poison emanated during the churning of the milk ocean by the devatas and daityas, it was Lord Shiva who stopped it from spreading by cupping all that poison in his hands and drinking it. It indicates that he is ready to take on great personal inconveniences for the sake of the welfare of the world. Sometimes he appears as Mahakal from a chasm in the earth to reciprocate the faith shown by his devotees. Sometimes he takes the name of his devotee, like Ghushma, to be known as Ghushmeshwar. In his eagerness to see the child form of Lord Krishna, he travels as a yogi to Vrindavan and visits Ayodhya as an astrologer to see Lord Rama's childhood. Thus, he is also known as the greatest devotee of the Lord and is proclaimed to be famously Vaishnavanam yatha shambhuh.

nimna-gānāṁ yathā gaṅgā
devānām acyuto yathā
vaiṣṇavānāṁ yathā śambhuḥ
purāṇānām idam tathā

Amongst rivers, Ganga is the greatest. Amongst deities, Lord Achyuta. Amongst Vaishnavas, it is Lord Shambhu, and amongst Puranas, Shrimad Bhagavatam.

[*Srimad Bhagavatam* 12.13.16]

This book, *Shiva*, is a compilation of wonderful tales giving insights into many temples and many names of Shiva, sourced from ancient texts like the Shiva Purana, Vishnu Purana, Matsya Purana, the Mahabharata, Srimad Bhagavatam, Tulsidas Ramcharitmanasa, and even folk tales. So, open any story from this wonderful repertoire of Shiva lilas and let your consciousness be helplessly dragged into this nectarine vision of Lord Shiva. Feel yourself enclosed in a cocoon of joy as each tale transports you to a newer discovery of this wonderful personality, Shiva!

Dr Shubha Vilas

Contents

1

KAILASH
A Fascinating Creation

Sage Narada had a persistent question in his mind ever since he came back from Mount Kailash. How did such an enthralling place come to be? There must be a narrative behind it that is equally intriguing. Brahma, his father, would be the best one to provide such details.Very soon Narada found himself seated at Brahma's feet, engrossed in the fascinating age old story.

Brahma took Narada to Kampilyanagar, where Yajnadutt, a brahmin, lived with his wife and son Gunanidhi. Even though the father was a skilled priest who meticulously performed the intricate Soma yajnas, his son was living in a different reality. He had little interest in religion or rituals. He was naturally prone to the sinful ways of life and loved gambling.

Gunanidhi's mother knew of her son's addictions but she ensured that her husband never got an inkling of their son's dependences. The mother's protection made him more confident, and soon he gambled away all their valuables.

It just so happened that Yajnadutt saw his ring on the finger of a notorius village gambler one day. When confronted, the gambler revealed that Gunanidhi was the one who had lost the ring and numerous other valuables in his gambling spree.

The grieving father simply left after learning of his son's transgressions and how his wife had encouraged him on the path to his miserable existence. After his father left, Gunanidhi was stunned.

With no support and a deep sense of guilt for breaking his wonderful family, he set out cursing his fate.

He walked aimlessly for days together. Hunger and thirst mauled him. He couldn't walk any further. Weakness overtook his sadness. Just then, he spotted a group of people walking towards a temple with offerings of food for the holy deities of the temple. Unable to withstand his hunger, Gunanidhi sneaked into the group and walked along with them to the temple. He waited for the right time till everyone was fast asleep.

Once he was sure that no one would spot him stealing the food left at the altar, he walked over the sleeping bodies of the devotees and pushed open the sanctum door. The only lamp that was burning inside the altar was almost on the verge of extinguishing.

Before the room plunged into complete darkness, Gunanidhi tore some of his cloth and rolled it into a wick, then lit the lamp. With enough light to see all the offerings, he filled his hands with as much as he could hold. Turning around, he sneaked out of the inner sanctum.

Unfortunately for him, one of the sleeping devotees was struck by his foot. The alert devotee immediately raised an alarm, and everyone present there, assuming he was a thief stealing the deities' jewellery, pounced on him and they beat him to pulp. Already weak, Gunanidhi couldn't handle the beating and died within a few minutes of being thrashed by the angry mob.

The Yamadutas arrived to claim Gunanidhi's soul after his death in the ethereal realm, and cast him into a hellish existence. They were shocked to see the powerful Shivaganas arrive there at that same moment. The Yamadutas were shocked to see them claiming the soul of such a sinful wretch—Gunanidhi.

The Shivaganas explained that, they were correct, but there was one detail that they had overlooked. The night he died happened to be Shivaratri, and he had unknowingly fasted all day, participated in the festival at the temple, and even lit a lamp at the altar of Lord Shiva. Even though all of this was done unknowingly, he would still get the benefit of it and be reborn as the king of Kalinga in his next birth to continue his devotion to Lord Shiva.

Accordingly, in his next life, he was born as Dama, the son of the King of Kalinga. When his father, King Arindam, died, he succeeded him and inspired thousands to take up the worship of Lord Shiva. He also renovated numerous temples and increased the standard of worship in all temples.

Thus, the sinful Gunanidhi became one of the foremost devotees of Lord Shiva. Eventually, during the *Padma kalpa**, Sage Vishrawas was born to Pulatsya Muni and begot the same Gunanidhi as his son. Inspired by his father's meditation, Gunanidhi practiced tremendous austerities for aeons together.

Finally pleased with his sincerity, Lord Shiva appeared to him along with Parvati. The only boon Gunanidhi wanted

---

* The last Kalpa, the ending day of the 50th year is called Padma Kalpa.

was to always be close to Shiva. This request really pleased Lord Shiva. But somehow Parvati wasn't so happy with Gunanidhi because she felt that he was staring at her with angry eyes.

It was indeed true that Gunanidhi was upset with Parvati. In fact, he was jealous that she was always able to accompany Shiva everywhere and had such proximity to him. She gave him the name "Kubera", which means one who is staring at her with angry eyes.

When Kubera returned to his father, Vishrawas, who was pleased with his devotion and mannerism, he offered him a place named Alkapuri as his residence. Keeping his promise, Lord Shiva then ordered Vishwakarma, the celestial architect, to construct an abode right next to Kubera's residence so that he would always be in close proximity to his favourite devotee.

Thus, Kubera had full access to Kailash and to his master, Lord Shiva. Eventually, he was appointed the treasurer of the gods. The life of Gunanidhi is a sparkling example of what one can achieve if one follows a spiritual path with all sincerity.

2

Avadhuta Shiva

Right at the entrance of Kailash was a very strange-looking person. Never before had Indra and Brihaspati seen anyone like him. They had paid many visits to Lord Shiva in Kailash. But this was a strange experience.

The rugged man standing before them was stark naked but had a fierce look on his face. He had the lustre of a blazing fire. He stood menacingly, blocking their way. He had long, matted hair that hung coarsely around his head, partially covering his face. Even then, his glowing reddish eyes were clearly visible and seemed threatening.

Indra began conversing with him to figure out what his intention was. He asked the gigantic personality in a tone that wasn't exactly respectful, "Who are you, Avadhuta? Where have you come from? What is your name? Better answer my questions truthfully. Is Lord Shiva in his abode? Is he out somewhere? I have come here with my guru to see him on behalf of the gods."

Indra asked so many questions, but the answer was pin-drop silence. Of course, it wasn't exactly complete silence. The icy cold winds that blew across the Kailash mountains seemed to match the Avadhuta's mood, who stood motionless. Except for his eyes that moved and his hair that waved in the wind, there was no other movement.

Indra repeated his questions, only to meet the steely, silent stares of the Avadhuta. It was almost as if his silence was a form of provocation. And Indra was indeed getting provoked. No one had ever ignored him like this. After all, he was the king of the heavens, and he deserved all the respect.

The furious Indra rebuked the naked Avadhuta in an attempt to shake him out of his eerie silence. "You fool! How dare you not answer my questions? Even though I am repeatedly asking you, you have the audacity to remain quiet, testing my patience. You deserve death as a punishment for your misconduct with the king of the heavens. My thunderbolt weapon will teach you a lesson that no one has taught you thus far. Wicked Avadhuta, call anyone you want to protect you from my wrath. Let me see who comes to your rescue now."

Summoning his thunderbolt, Indra stared at the silent spectator in fury. With the weapon raised in the air and his anger out of control, Indra was about to hurl the weapon at the offender. He placed himself one step ahead, getting into an attacking stance, and tried to release the thunderbolt at the perceived enemy.

Suddenly, he realised that his hand was frozen. Try as he might, he just couldn't budge his arm. In fact, his entire right shoulder had frozen along with his arm. It definitely wasn't due to the chilling cold of Kailash. It had something to do with the cold stare of the Avadhuta.

Seeing Indra frozen, Brihaspati, who had thus far been quiet, realised that if he did not step in now, it could be the end for Indra. The Avadhuta was glaring with great anger at the helplessly struggling Indra. His eyes blazed with dazzling brilliance. Something most astounding happened just then. The forehead of Avadhuta opened up, and a third eye shone from there. Brihaspati ran forward and prostrated himself on the floor in front of the naked personality who was about to burn Indra down. Brihaspati began to offer serious prayers, beseeching him.

By now, it was obvious that this Avadhuta was none other than Lord Shiva himself, who had appeared in that form to test them. And they had failed miserably in that test. Now they were about to face dire consequences. Of all the many prayers that Brihaspati offered to appease Lord Shiva, two struck the right chords. One was that he addressed Lord Shiva as the husband of Gauri, and the second was that he addressed him as the Lord of the distressed. Lord Shiva softened when he remembered his wife Gauri, and he thawed even more when he was reminded of his soft-hearted nature of being compassionate to those in need.

When Brihaspati saw that his prayers were having the desired effect, he continued glorifying the Lord with the best of prayers. In the meanwhile, he cleverly helped Indra fall to his feet even though his one arm was still frozen. Though very uncomfortable, Indra fell to the ground, touched his head to the cold floor of the Kailash Mountains, and joined in the prayers, asking Lord Shiva's forgiveness for his arrogance. He realised that, though he was the king of the heavens, he had no right to display arrogance in Kailash. He shouldn't have judged someone just by their appearance. His sincere words of repentance melted Lord Shiva's heart, and he began to laugh out loudly.

Shiva spoke with a voice booming like a thunderclap. "How do you expect me to hold the fire that has come out of my third eye out of great anger? How can I not release it now?"

With great humility, Brihaspati said, "My dear Lord, your name is Bhaktavatsala. Anyone who has sought refuge in you cannot be lost. Indra has sought refuge in you and is repenting for his mistake. Kindly cast away that angry spell elsewhere and spare Indra's life."

Shiva smiled at Brihaspati's humble request. He blessed the guru of the gods with a new name, Jiva. He said, "Because you saved the life of Indra, you will be famous as Jiva. I am pleased with you and bless you. I will cast this fire into the ocean and ensure that it doesn't affect Indra."

Shiva turned towards the south. Immediately, a ball of fire bolted out from his third eye and sped towards the sea. As soon as that ball of fire fell into the sea, a child was born there. This son, who was born from the angry vision of Shiva, eventually came to be known as Jalandhara. He was also called Sindhuputra, the son of the ocean.

The moment the third eye closed, the Avadhuta form of Lord Shiva disappeared. Indra's frozen hand got reactivated. Brihaspati and Indra offered their obeisance to the abode of Lord Shiva and quickly escaped from there, not wanting any more adventure for the day.

They glorified this incarnation of Lord Shiva as Avadhuteshwar and shared their experience with the whole world. Indra was not ashamed to admit that he was badly defeated by the mere stare of Lord Shiva. Thus, Avadhuteshwar became a name that got eternally associated with Lord Shiva.

3

Daksha Shiva Conflict

Lord Shiva hurried to reach Prayag on time. He did not want to be labelled a latecomer for the massive *yagya* held by Brahmadeva at the holy Triveni Sangam. Being an important sacrifice for the welfare of the world, Brahmadeva had sent out invitations to all devatas and his manas-putras, the mind-born sons. Daksha, his son, and Prajapati were his most important guests.

As soon as Daksha walked in, everyone in the assembly hall stood up respectfully. As Prajapati, he commanded the respect of devatas. Daksha's chest swelled up with pride as he looked around the assembly hall. He did a quick survey to ensure that all were standing up in reverence! He was, after all, the Prajapati—the head of the universal family. Not to forget, also the son of Brahmadeva. It was therefore mandatory for everyone to pay their respects to him.

His eyes darted to and fro, glad to see that everyone understood the gravity of his position. His entry had brought everyone to their feet. He smiled at Brahmadeva, his father, who of course had no reason to stand up. Brahmadeva smiled back fondly at Daksha and signalled for him to sit.

As he was about to take his seat, his eyes fell on Lord Shiva. Lord Shiva had the audacity to remain seated in Daksha's presence. It really incensed Daksha to no end to see such disrespect meted out to him. He could excuse Brahma for being seated, but he could definitely not accept Shiva being seated. Daksha, like any other person used to receiving honour, feared dishonour the most.

To make matters worse, Shiva was not even looking towards Daksha. He seemed to be in a world of his own, oblivious to what was happening around him. Oblivious to the hateful fireballs bouncing from Daksha's eyes.

Daksha's blood was boiling at Shiva's blatant breach of conduct. As his anger rose to a zenith, he threw self-control out the window and spat out words more poisonous than snake venom. If words could kill, not just Shiva but the entire assembly of devatas would have fallen dead in a heap.

"When one and all bow before me, only this wicked man sits in defiance."

Devatas were horrified to hear Daksha's vile speech. They shrank back, terrified of his rage, anticipating a curse to fall on them too.

"I curse him that he will no longer be allowed to partake in any yagya offerings."

Such rage had taken hold of Daksha that his intelligence and sanity deserted him. Too shocked to even move a finger, everyone watched the scene unfold in front of them, gasping at the implications of the curse.

The first one to finally move and react was none other than the loyal Nandi.

"O' Daksha, how foolish can you be? Cursing Lord Shiva? Curses do not have any effect on him."

Nandi knew his master well. He was indifferent and far away from mundane emotions like hurt and anger, respect and disrespect. His master was always immersed in meditation and had probably not even noticed the arrival of Daksha. And even if he had, he would have remained seated to protect Daksha. If he stood up, Daksha would surely fall down.

But there was no use explaining these intricate aspects to someone who was bereft of all sensibilities. So, Nandi tried to explain the futility of cursing Lord Shiva. Not that he expected Daksha to understand in his fit of insanity.

Daksha turned his rage towards Nandi. Anyone who obstructed his path would become the target of his wrath.

"I curse all followers of Shiva to be excluded from all Vedic ceremonies," stuttered Daksha in a single breath, "no one will ever be invited again. No brahman will perform a sacrifice for you. You will spend your days in intoxication, just like your master."

Nandi now lost it. He yelled back at him, "Whoever curses Lord Shiva will become a beggar and incapable of performing heavenly yagyas. And you, particularly, will suffer and regret your sins." Nandi said this with his body trembling and his finger pointing to Daksha.

Not wanting to prolong everyone's agony, Shiva walked out of the hall. His followers, taking his cue, emptied the hall, leaving behind a very shaken gathering of invitees.

But that was not the end as far as Daksha was concerned. He had been insulted, and he did not take insults lightly. Definitely not from the ascetic Shiva. He never liked his son-in-law, but the dislike had taken deeper roots now. He would teach him a lesson. He would take revenge for the dishonour he had faced at the hands of Shiva. He didn't care about his daughter, Sati, anymore. Too bad for Sati that she was Shiva's wife. Sati had lost the right to even be called his daughter. She, too, was his enemy. The friend of an enemy was also an enemy. And they'd both pay the price.

Daksha left the yagya, his head full of plans for how he would disrespect Shiva and get even with him. It was only a matter of time. He finally allowed himself a smile, knowing what he would do next.

4

Sati's Test

"I can't believe this!" she said, nodding her head in utter disbelief. "Trust me, dear. I can clearly read your mind. What you are thinking of is nothing short of madness. Don't take such a risk!" He tried to be kind, yet firm. What his wife was getting into was enormously risky! He had to dissuade her.

She was adamant. To begin with, she never thought it was a risk at all. She was convinced that her husband was getting worked up for no real reason. She wasn't going to believe something was real just because everyone was saying so. Even if everyone included her learned husband, Lord Shiva. Detached as he was, Shiva silently left the arena of trouble, allowing his wife to take the knocks and find out for herself. Some things are best learned through personal experience.

The scene below was as it had been a few minutes ago. Rama was still crying, and his brother Lakshmana was still silently following him, a little distance away, all the while on the lookout for Sita. Sita had been kidnapped by Ravana, and the two brothers were desperately looking for her. Rama was totally disheartened and was crying intensely while calling out to his beloved wife.

This was the scene that met the eyes of Shiva and Sati when they were incidentally passing by the forest close to Panchavati. Sati was shocked that the Supreme Lord could be so disturbed by the loss of his wife. How could the all-knowing person be so perturbed?

There was only one way to decipher the truth. An illusion check! The next minute, she was no longer Sati, the wife of Lord Shiva, but Sita, the wife of Lord Rama.

As Rama wobbled into that area, calling out to Sita with overwhelming emotions, she came out from her hiding place and presented herself. She looked down shyly. Yet at the same time, she made sure to keep a tab on his initial reactions. What transpired in the next few moments sent a shiver down her spine!

One moment, he was a teary-eyed and worried husband who had lost his wife. The next, he was a sober, regal, and extremely gentlemanly prince. Standing erect with folded hands and veneration filled eyes, he said something that shocked her.

"What are you doing here alone in the middle of this dangerous forest, Mother Sati? Where is Lord Shiva? Why hasn't he accompanied you on this journey?"

How could this be? How could he recognise her in this disguise? She was supposed to be illusory energy personified. No one had ever been able to see through her flawless illusions and tricks. She looked at herself once again just to be sure that the disguise had not faded away. Everything was perfect. There was no way anyone could have felt that she was not Sita. Every feature of Sita's persona was flawlessly visible, even to the minutest mannerism.

"Hmm . . . Hmm . . ." No words came out of her mouth. Actually, there was nothing to say. Actions had spoken louder than words—both their actions.

In Kailash, she was greeted by a cold gust of wind. She couldn't share her findings with her husband as he was engaged in fierce meditation. He never saw her again. After this episode, Sati went to her father Daksha's house, where he severely insulted her husband, Shiva. Unable to take the insult of her husband, she self-immolated and gave up her body.

Eventually, in her next life, she became Parvati and was married to Shiva again. Because Sati had taken the form of Sita, whom Shiva considered to be his worshipable mother, he did not want to associate with her anymore as his wife.

5

Sati Pays the Price

Ever since Shiva had come back from the yagya, Sati had been filled with a sense of foreboding. She couldn't quite place her finger on what was wrong. Shiva, as usual, was hardly around, immersed in meditation. There was no one who could understand or explain why she felt the way she did—as if a catastrophe was waiting to happen. She decided to wait for her Lord to come back to external consciousness.

It was a beautiful day, and as Sati looked up at the sky, she saw celestial beings hurrying towards their destinations. This was something unusual. Never had she seen so much aerial traffic. It looked as if everyone had been invited to some spectacular event. But how could that be?

That there was a spectacular event that she was not just left out of but did not even know about it . . . *highly improbable*, she muttered to herself. She continued looking at the sky for clues about where everyone was going. But she could only make out that everyone was well dressed and excited. Everyone wanted to be on time for what appeared to be something sensational.

Disappointed, she went to check on Shiva to see if he could be of any help. Fortunately for her, he stirred. She sat next to him, waiting for more movements from him. Her presence would prompt him to stop his meditation, knowing that she needed him.

Lord Shiva, though in meditation, knew exactly what was going on. Sensing Sati's anxiety and restlessness, he decided to do what was necessary to help Sati. After all, he was responsible for all that was going on. As soon as he opened his eyes, he was surrounded by Sati's two eyes. Her eyes were imploring him to fill in the gaps in her understanding.

Shiva took a deep breath and said, "Everyone is going to attend a sacrificial ceremony at your father, Daksha's house. It is a big event."

As expected by Shiva, Sati gasped, "How can it be that my father has organised an event and not invited us?"

"He has not called us because he wants to take revenge by insulting me." Shiva's calm voice betrayed no emotions.

He explained to Sati how Daksha had been offended and insulted when Shiva remained seated at the yagya. Sati, although miffed at her father for his unexpected tantrums, was still mortified at being left out of a family event. It was her family, her house . . . and she had been excluded. As she saw the flurry of activity in the sky, she had a sudden thought, which she shared with her husband.

"Do I really need an invitation to go to my own house? I can go anytime I want, can't I?" She looked at him, her eyes pleading for him to agree with her sentiments.

Not wanting to agitate her further, he replied, "It is not advisable to go anywhere uninvited. Because you are my wife, they will disrespect you too. I don't want you to get hurt and then react in anger. So, my advice, dear Sati, is to stay home."

Sati could not stop the tears from rolling down her cheeks. She couldn't imagine how her loving family could misbehave with her. She was their darling daughter. Her restlessness was growing with every passing moment, knowing that everyone—other than her—was heading to her parent's house.

Unable to bear the torture anymore, she declared, "I will go for sure because I don't mind going home uninvited."

Shiva did not try to stop her. All he said was, "You are mature enough to make your decisions. But please remember that if they disrespect you, you should, control your anger. If you fail to tolerate the insults, you may come to harm."

Sati did not realise how prophetic Lord Shiva's words were. She left happily, accompanied by Nandi, the white bull.

When she reached the yagya, she saw her entire family assembled there. She spotted her father and went to greet him. Daksha, however, displayed his unhappiness at her appearance and spoke displeasing words about Shiva.

"Shiva is unworthy of being invited to this yagya. He is evil and inauspicious, smeared with ash from crematoriums."

Sati felt extremely hurt by this unnecessary verbal assault on her husband. She pleaded with him to stop using such language, but Daksha was determined to vent his rage on Sati, who represented Shiva.

"He is clothed like a beggar and dances like a madman . . ."

Sati blanked out, unable to continue hearing more vile words. Shiva's words rang in her ears.

"Control your anger. If you fail to tolerate the insults, you may come to harm."

As the echo of the words became stronger and stronger, Sati decided to denounce her father and let herself be consumed in the fire. She preferred to be born again, this time to another father whom she could respect. In front of the entire world seated in the hall, Sati burst into a ball of fire and ended her life.

Nandi had to break the sad news to Shiva—of Sati leaving her body. The news left Shiva in immense pain. He cried out loud, shaking the entire universe. He would not allow Daksha to go scot-free this time. Revenge he would take for sure. For that, he created a demon Virbhadra from his matted hair. Next, he created a powerful army of demons to accompany Virbhadra.

The powerful attack deflated Daksha's ego. Terrified to see the size of Virbhadra, he sought shelter from Vishnu, but Vishnu chastised him for his foolishness. Daksha had played with fire and would have to suffer the consequences. Virbhadra destroyed everything that came in his way, slaying Daksha and his followers.

Shiva's anger was such that the entire universe was on the brink of destruction. Vishnu ordered all the devatas to apologise to Shiva and calm him down. Finally, Shiva relented, and the devatas asked him to revive Daksha. Shiva asked Bhrigu to bring a goat's head, which he attached to Daksha's body.

A grateful Daksha sprang back to life and fell at Shiva's feet. Regretting his mistakes, Daksha offered heartfelt prayers to Shiva and ended the bitter battle. The yagya continued, but this time in the presence of Lord Shiva and with his blessings.

Shiva then returned to his meditation to await the rebirth of Sati and unite with her again.

6

The Story of Love, Hope, and Peace

While Shiva burned in the fire of meditation, the rest of the devatas burned in the fire of revenge. Revenge against the demon Tarakasura. While Shiva sat peacefully in his cave, the devatas had been dislodged from their heavenly abodes by the near-immortal demon.

This demon, Tarakasura was born from the union of princess Maya and sage Kashyap. Simhamugan and Surpadman were his brothers, and Ajamukhi was his sister. They all had one goal. To humble the gods and dominate the three worlds. They spent innumerable years in penance to please Lord Shiva. Again, with a single-point agenda—to gain so much power that they could take over heaven, earth, and hell.

Surely Shiva would help by granting them a boon.

"Please bless us with the boon that we can be killed only and only by your own Shakti and no one else."

Shiva was unconcerned about the boons that were constantly being asked of him. He simply granted them whatever they wanted and disappeared, leaving behind the supremely ecstatic trio of demon brothers.

They had been cunning enough in asking him for a boon that would not be denied. They did not ask for immortality. Instead, they asked to be killed by Shiva's Shakti. They were well aware that Sati had departed, and the chances of Shiva marrying again were next to impossible. This meant that the possibility of their killer being born was also remote.

Convinced that they would remain invincible and eternal, they planned to crown themselves as the undisputed kings of the entire universe.

It did not take much effort to drive away the devatas from the heavenly planets.

The dejected devatas lost unceremoniously and desperately needed a commander-in-chief who could lead them to victory and help regain their kingdom as well as their pride. They were headless at the moment.

Taking shelter in Lord Brahma was a way of life for them. This time too, they beseeched Brahma to help them fight the demon family. Brahma, the embodiment of wisdom, as usual, knew exactly what the problem was and how it could be solved.

"You can defeat the demons if Shiva can father a warrior."

But alas, Shiva had gone into seclusion after losing Sati. Brahma's solution failed to inspire the *devatas*. Shiva had no intention of tying the knot ever again. Would that mean no one could bring down Tarakasura? Would they never reclaim heaven again? The future certainly looked uncertain and bleak.

Meanwhile, destiny was playing its role. Parvati, a beautiful girl child, was born to Queen Meena, wife of King Himvat of the Himalayas. The word 'Parvati' meant 'belonging to the hill'. This child was full of life, and her determination was as strong as her mountainous heritage.

Since childhood, she had a great attraction for Lord Shiva, spending hours together praying to him instead of playing with her friends. This did not change a bit, even as she grew older. Her attraction for him only escalated with time.

One day Narada muni paid a visit. In an instant, he knew the burning desire inside Parvati to obtain Shiva as her life partner. Becoming her spiritual master, he advised her to engage in severe penance to please Lord Shiva. Surely, once pleased, he would fulfil her wish.

Without any hesitation, Parvati eagerly followed Narada muni's instructions. Secretly, she was happy that someone understood her and encouraged her. Her parents were in the dark. But she would cross that bridge later. For now, her goal was to impress Lord Shiva with her austerities so that he would accept her.

She started the process in earnest, but soon she was disturbed by the Saptarishis, the seven exalted sages. The path to obtain God was never easy. The Saptarishis wanted to test her sincerity. Did she really want to marry Shiva? How determined was she? Would she give up if Shiva did not appear? Their plan was to dissuade her and see her response.

"Dear maiden, daughter of the Himalayas, we heard Narada muni has instigated you to do *tapasya* to obtain Lord Shiva. But we came to put some sense into you. Lord Shiva is an ascetic and will remain an ascetic. He is hardly the kind of person you can be happy with. Vishnu is a much better option for you. It is foolishness to take advice from Narada muni of all people; he can only give you advice on how to remain unmarried."

This was a real test for Parvati. A test of her faith and resilience. Would she cave in or would she stand firm? Parvati was faith personified, and the first symptom of faith is determination. To remain unaffected by fear or temptation. The Saptarishis were tempting her to give up her austerities.

Parvati replied, "One who gives up her goal because of others' opinions will never achieve anything worthwhile in life."

"You are proving yourself to be the daughter of the mountain by showing your gross (stone-like) intelligence and choosing Narada muni as your spiritual master,", the test continued.

Parvati defended herself, saying "If I have gross intelligence, how do you expect me to change my mind? Gold is found in dirt and even after being purified, it does not let go of its properties. Then how can you expect me to change my mind? My heart does not analyse whether Vishnu is more suitable. It is Shiva who I desire and it is not easy to understand why one is attracted to a particular person."

She further asserted her faith in Narada muni. "I have full faith in Narada muni's words. If you cannot have faith in your spiritual master, how can you hope to achieve anything? Even if Lord Shiva himself comes to stop me from following Narada muni's path, I will not be swayed. I have but one desire; even after taking birth one crore times, I will only want Lord Shiva as my husband. No one else but him."

Thus, Parvati gave the seven sages a lesson on spirituality. The secret of every spiritualist is that, however important the goal may be, the role of the guru is always higher. Only the guru has the power to connect us to the goal when we think it is out of reach.

Quietly pleased with her unshakeable resolve, the seven sages left. Parvati had passed the first test. Far away, hidden in his cave, Shiva was still immersed in his inner world, meditating upon higher truths. Devatas had waited patiently for him to end his reverie and hear their plea.

They desperately needed a child from him to defeat the evil forces. Indra decided it was time to give up the wait and take an active step to shake Shiva out of his world. Parvati was already doing her best to attain Shiva. If he could get them together, their problem would be solved.

He summoned Kamadeva, the god of love. If he could shoot his love arrows at Shiva, love would blossom easily, paving the path for marriage and eventually a child.

But when Kamadeva heard the sinister proposal, he shivered in fear. What if Shiva saw him? What if he got caught? He would surely lose his life. Indra was in no mood to listen to his fears. He instructed him to approach Shiva along with his wife Rati and Vasanta and do the needful to help the devatas.

Kama left, not too happy with the suicidal task handed out to him. With Rati and Vasanta in tow, they reached Lord Shiva. The arrival of Vasanta (also known as the spring season) immediately changed the icy cold landscape into an exquisite panorama.

Flowers in rainbow hues sprung up, spreading their delightful fragrance. The cool breeze hurried to spread the fragrance far and wide. Earth was like a dressed-up bride brimming with flowery ornaments. Juicy fruits hung low, kissing the ground. Bees buzzed around flowers intoxicated with sweet nectar, and *koyals* cooed, igniting flames of love in many hearts. Waterfalls and rivers added to the merriment with joyful sounds as they rubbed shoulders with the mountains. Romance was in the air. No one could possibly escape the effects of something as powerful as this.

Having set the scene, Kamadeva found a suitable position in Shiva's vicinity to shoot the arrow at him. If all went well, Shiva would wake up in a love filled environment, yearning to unite with Parvati. And if something went wrong . . . Kamadeva shuddered to think what would happen.

Gathering all his courage, he shot from his love bow. The arrow, dipped in desire, left Kamadeva and went straight to Shiva's heart. Indra and his entourage watched in great anticipation, praying for the love magic to work.

Soon enough, something stirred within Shiva. He felt a strange feeling overpowering his senses and spreading outwards from his heart. His heart fluttered and a wave of excitement swept his being. The environment was most conducive to some light-heartedness.

He saw Parvati meditating on him, and his heart missed a beat. Till now, he had ignored her, not really wanting to get entangled again. But today, he simply wanted to hold her in his arms. She was so pretty and vivacious that he just had to invite her over.

As he looked around, drinking in the beauty of nature, something caught his eye. A movement behind a tree.

On closer scrutiny, he found it was Kamadeva. Was it a coincidence that he felt overwhelming love for Parvati when Kamadeva was around? Surely not.

Putting two and two together, Shiva flew into a rage. His third eye opened automatically, and he looked hard at Kamadeva. A fire shot out and engulfed the god of love. Shiva's chilling stare had reduced Kamadeva to a handful of ash in one instance.

As soon as Kamadeva was destroyed, a cloud of gloom hung over the world. How could the world exist if every living being's desires and love were drained away? Love was slowly replaced by hatred and revenge. Unable to withstand the toxic environment saturated with malice and spite, flowers, trees, and all vegetation ceased. Green landscapes gave way to gloomy grey.

Rati stood shell-shocked, watching the horrifying scene. She ran towards Shiva, begging for forgiveness. How could he be so hard-hearted? She sobbed and asked him to bring Kamadeva back for her. Rati was so badly affected that her sad state moved Shiva, and he pronounced that Kamadeva would be born as Krishna's son. In the Dwapara yuga, Rati took birth again to claim her husband, who appeared as Sri Krishna's son Pradyumna.

After Kamadeva was burnt to ashes, the seven sages went back to Parvati to convey the bad news. Without Kama, how could she ever hope to have Shiva's love? They narrated Kamadeva's efforts with sarcasm and bluntly concluded that she would never be able to entice Shiva without Kamadeva.

But Parvati's answer touched them deeply. She was not just determined to reach her goal; she was intelligent too. She said, "Do you believe that Shiva has been able to destroy his desires only now? Don't you know that he is eternally free from desire? I have worshipped Mahadeva knowing him to be without any material desires and without any need for sense gratification. I have full faith that Shiva will accept me even then."

Parvati again checkmated the seven sages. Kamadeva going up in smoke was neither astonishing, nor unexpected. Shiva, to her, was eternally devoid of desires. There was no change in her expectations after hearing the news that the seven sages had given her. True faith is not based on expectations. When Parvati stopped speaking, the sages bowed down to her and disappeared.

Shiva, even without Kamadeva's love shot, was truly in love with Parvati. He proposed to her, and Parvati gladly accepted, bringing smiles to the devatas' sulky faces. A grand wedding took place in the Himalayas, where Brahma played the role of the priest and Vishnu, as her brother, gave Parvati's hand to Shiva.

The entire universe waited patiently for the arrival of Shiva and Parvati's child, who would lead them to victory against Tarakasura and his brothers. It turned out to be a long, long wait as Shiva and Parvati transported themselves to a private world of love. Thousands of years passed by. Unable to wait any longer, the gods prayed to Lord Shiva to give them a child to end their misery.

Shiva finally heard them and released his Shakti for the gods. It was so potent that no one had the capacity to handle it. Agni came forward to catch the potency but it was too hot even for him to handle. Agni himself felt too hot holding it in his hands. Shiva told him to deposit it with women who bathe in the early hours of Magha.

Agni hurried to find them and found the wives of the seven sages bathing. After their bath, they were all shivering and wanted to warm their hands in the fire. Arundhati, wife of sage Vasishta, tried to stop them, but they were under the spell of Lord Shiva. They insisted on going near the fire.

Immediately, particles of the potent semen entered their bodies, which in turn relieved Agni from the agonising pain. The embryo inside the women turned on the heat, putting them in intense distress. Their restlessness and pain slowly increased, reaching a peak.

Not knowing what to do, they rushed to Himvat and aborted the embryo there. Scorched by the hot embryos, Himvat hurled them into the Ganga. Ganga too could not bear the potent heat and deposited it in the Sara Forest, where the child eventually was born.

As soon as the child opened his eyes, celestial music echoed from the sky. The air was filled with the sounds of drums and tambourines. Parvati and Shiva became joyous at the arrival of their handsome son. Signs of auspiciousness cropped up around the world. The wicked demons would now see darkness. The gods rejoiced as they saw the end of their agony approaching.

The child was named Kartikeya and made the commander-in-chief of the gods because of his astute abilities in war. Soon enough, they were attacked by *asuras* led by Taraka. Their antics and thumping shook the earth. Their war cries jolted the entire universe. This time the gods were ready. They had Kartikeya to lead them to victory.

A splendorous chariot arrived for Kartikeya. Varuna presented him with a lustrous umbrella overhead, dazzling with diamonds. Other gods joined him with their own forces. Both sides were eager to attack and crush each other. A fierce battle erupted, and in no time, the battleground was strewn with heads, trunks, and limbs.

Blood flowed abundantly, attracting ghosts and goblins. Agni, Yama, Varuna, Vayu, and Chandra fought against Samhrada, Bala, Suvira, Sumbha, and Kumbha. *Suras* and *asuras* fought one-on-one with great resoluteness. The fight suddenly took a turn when Indra was hit by a spear and fell from his elephant. Demotivated by this, one by one, other suras fell too. Their powers could not match the fury of the demons.

Angered by the turn of events, Virbhadra threw his trident at Taraka. The surprise attack knocked him unconscious. He was up again in a jiffy to counterattack his assailant. One after another, they threw the deadliest weapons as others gazed at them in fear. The *ganas*, encouraged by their leader, escalated their attack. Taraka assumed a hundred hands to quell the resurgence. Now, it was time for Kartikeya to enter the scene.

It was a fight the gods would remember as long as they lived. The two fought like wounded lions. They attacked with weapons, they fought bare-handed, and they wounded each other; blood flowed profusely from their faces, arms, and legs, but there was no stopping them.

Kartikeya wondered how he would ever kill the invincible Taraka. None of his powerful missiles were effective. The celestials watching the battle had only one question—who will win?

From the corner of his eye, Kartikeya saw Vishnu near him. The secret to killing Taraka, Vishnu revealed, was to break the *atmalingam* around his neck. Relieved to know the source of his strength, Kartikeya struck his divine spear, which broke apart the lingam into five pieces. The broken lingam brought Taraka down, and he finally fell to the ground in anguish. The heroic Kartikeya had executed his job to perfection. The other asuras who were still alive fled from there.

The universe had been freed from prickly thorn-like demons. The gods were celebrating. Shiva and Parvati appeared and fondled their son lovingly amidst cheers of victory. All was well in the three worlds once again.

7

Chandrashekhar Shiva

Haryashvas and Savalashvas had gone against their father Daksha's wishes and decided not to get married and to live a life of devotion. This was greatly disappointing for Daksha, the progenitor of mankind. Badly let down by his sons, his wife Prasuti and he then decided to have only daughters. As a result, sixty-two daughters were born. Twenty-seven of these daughters were eventually wedded to Chandradeva (the Moon god).

Chandra, who was already so handsome, became more effulgent and radiant when surrounded by his twenty-seven beautiful wives. His dark brown lustrous locks added to his charm. One could easily drown in the pools of his ocean-blue eyes. And when he walked, he was as radiant as millions of diamonds. Who could resist his charms as he glided across the sky, scattering cool moonlight on the surface of the earth?

Out of his twenty-seven wives, there was only one who could match his talents and charm, and that was Rohini. Her exquisite beauty led Chandra to frenzied excitement, and he endeavoured to spend all his time in her exotic company. He also bestowed special favours on her, completely neglecting his other wives.

This supremely attractive moon god, though, had one fault. He was not at all an easy person to get along with. The neglected wives felt abandoned and insulted, and when they could not tolerate their husband's blazing preference for Rohini any longer, they had only one option left—present their case to their father, Daksha.

The twenty-six sisters together complained and vented out their frustrations in front of their powerful father, Daksha, so that he could prevail upon the erring Chandra. Daksha sympathised with his daughters and agreed to speak to Chandra and address his daughters' concerns.

Inviting Chandra home, Daksha advised him that he should give equal attention and importance to all his wives. Chandra heard him patiently, but did not change his ways. He continued to shower all his love on Rohini, unmindful of the consequences.

Since his advice was not taken seriously, Daksha was enraged. He did not like the injustice and humiliation his daughters were facing. To avenge them and teach Chandra a lesson, Daksha pronounced a curse on Chandra.

"Your radiance, brilliance, and good looks make you arrogant! Now you will lose all of it . . . no longer will anyone be attracted to you once you lose all your sheen."

Chandra was shell-shocked at the enormity of the curse. How could he even survive without his usual splendour? What's a moon without his moonlight? Without his cool radiance? He bent his head in shame and embarrassment as his effulgence slowly drained out, leaving him weak and emaciated.

When the sun went down, the naked sky was enveloped in an eerie darkness. No longer did the moon shine bright, enlivening the night. There were no waves in the ocean.

There was no taste in vegetables. Ashamed and embarrassed, the moon hid himself inside the ocean. As a result, the world was cloaked in darkness.

Taking advantage of the dark nights, evil forces became free to do as they liked. They roamed without fear, causing damage and destruction. *Rishis* and devatas were overwhelmed. Chandra was devastated and rapidly shrinking. His pathetically weak condition prompted Brahma to visit him. Brahma was moved to see Chandra's plight after being cursed. He offered him some advice.

"Why don't you meditate on Shiva? He can be easily pleased and can show you a way out."

Brahma's kind words lifted Chandra out of his gloom. He, immediately, departed to pray to Lord Shiva.He made a lingam on the banks of the River Saraswati at Prabhas tirtha. Months passed as Chandra meditated constantly on the Lord. So intense was his absorption that the entire Earth was burning in the heat of his penance. Shiva could no longer ignore him, and pleased with Chandra's sincerity in meditating for six long months, he appeared before him.

"What do you want from me, Chandra?" asked Shiva.

Chandra poured out his troubles to him, starting with his single-pointed attraction for Rohini and ending with the devastating curse from Daksha. He bared his heart and soul.

"Please, O' divine protector, save me from this meaningless existence. You are the shelter of one and all. You are the universal benefactor."

Shiva was moved by Chandra's sorry plight. He explained that no curse can be reversed in totality but can only be modified. Chandra again plunged into despair, losing all hope. Shiva smiled and extended his arm to pluck Chandra out of the sky and then tucked him nicely in his matted hair.

Chandra, surprised by Shiva's action, was delighted to experience strength and vigour, and his lost glory restored as soon as he found himself in contact with Shiva. As a rejuvenated Chandra beamed broadly from his new position, Shiva came to be known as Chandrashekhar, one who holds the crescent.

Shiva further prophesied that the moon would progressively grow stronger and brighter for the next fifteen days, and subsequently, he would lose his brilliance in the fortnight after that. This waxing and waning of the moon would continue eternally.

In this way, Lord Shiva was instrumental in founding the ancient Hindu calendar system based on the phases of the moon. A lunar month comprises two fortnights known as *Shukla paksha* (the bright phase) and *Krishna* paksha (the dark phase), or the waxing moon and waning moon.

Today, the lingam which Chandra prayed to is known as Somnath, the first of the *Jyotirlingams*. It is believed that Shiva is always present in that tirtha. The Somnath temple was built in gold by Chandradeva himself. Ashwayuja Purnima is one of the most auspicious days to worship Shiva.

On this day, Chandradeva comes closer to earth to worship Lord Shiva and inundates the earth with his spectacular luminescence. As per Shiva's boon, this is the only day the moon is in his full glory and the earth basks in dazzling moonlight. Devotees take the opportunity to thank Lord Shiva on this day for granting the full radiance of Chandradeva on earth.

Adi Parva in the *Mahabharata* reveals that Arjuna, assisted by Krishna, met Subhadra at this location and married her.

8

Who Is Nandi?

How unhappy Shilada was! He did not have a child he could love. His well-wishers advised him to pray to Indra and please him. If Indra was pleased, he would surely fulfil his desires. Shilada liked the idea. Only Indra, the king of heaven, could grant him the child he desired. He set off to the mountains with the hope in his heart that when he came back, he would be a happy man.

After a few years of austerity, Shilada succeeded in pleasing Indradeva. He was overjoyed to see the king of heaven standing before his eyes in all his glory. When Indra asked him what he could do for him, Shilada revealed his heart's desire.

"Please give me a son who is not born of a mother and lives forever."

Indra, who had been smiling till now, suddenly became grave.

"I do not have the authority to grant you what you wish for. Only Lord Shiva can help you," he replied, "please pray to him."

Saying this, Indra disappeared instantly.

A wee bit disappointed, Shilada continued his intense meditation. Hundreds of years passed, and he lost track of time. He would not stop till Lord Shiva appeared. He wanted to please him at any cost.

Because he had stopped eating and drinking, his body began to break down. He was now only a bag of bones. Ants and termites mistook him for a rock and built their homes on him. He was covered with ant hills, and insects were nibbling on his bones. Yet, his mind was absorbed in Shiva. Though Lord Shiva was supposed to be Ashutosh, the one who is easily pleased, he took very long to make his appearance.

Finally, Shilada's vibrations reached Lord Shiva in Kailash. He immediately appeared in front of his devotee. Lord Shiva touched him on his head, and Shilada felt a thrill of energy run through his body. His wounds healed as his flesh and muscles gained vigour once again. He sprang up and offered his obeisance to his Lord.

Though Shiva understood the desires of his devotees, he still preferred to hear it from them. Shiva encouraged him to speak from his heart. Shilada's words gushed out of his mouth, in anticipation of the boon.

"My Lord, please bless me with a child who is not born from a mother and who lives eternally."

"As you wish," said Shiva, "you may go back home and perform a yagya that will give you a child."

Before he could even react, Shiva disappeared in a flash, leaving behind a stunned Shilada. Once he came to his senses, Shilada hurried home to perform the yagya. To his shock and disbelief, out of the sacrificial fire emerged a young, strong lad clad in dazzling diamonds. How delighted Shilada was to see his dream materialise! He named the boy Nandi, which meant 'the one who is happy.'

Once Nandi stepped out of the sacrificial fire, he transformed into a normal boy. Gone were all the effulgence and the aura. No one could guess how extraordinary his birth had been. This boy turned out to be extremely brilliant and talented.

As he grew up, Shilada began educating him personally. He taught Nandi the *Vedas* and imparted all types of knowledge to him, ranging from medicine to dancing, from singing to arts, and from fighting to wisdom from sacred texts. Nandi was extraordinarily intelligent; he learned all of it in less than a fortnight.

One day, two powerful sages named Varun and Mitra visited Shilada. By this time. Nandi was seven years old. Shilada respectfully served them and took care of them. Then, at the opportune moment, he introduced his son Nandi to them. Nandi touched their feet to seek their blessings. But the colour on their faces vanished as soon as Nandi touched their feet.

Wanting to be honest with Shilada, the two sages explained to him that Nandi wouldn't live beyond a year. Shilada was broken-hearted to hear this prediction about the boy.

Once again, Shilada was pushed into a world of sorrow. Though he was badly shaken by this prediction, Nandi was totally unaffected. However, unable to see his father's pain, Nandi went to the Himalayas to appease Lord Shiva. Nandi had complete faith in Lord Shiva's prowess and his ability to reverse the flow of destiny.

Shiva appeared and gently revealed the truth to him: "Dear Nandi, you were originally in Kailash and were cursed by a muni to take birth as a human. It is now time for you to leave your human body and come back to your eternal spiritual form. You will always remain in my service, and the world will pray to you first, before entering my temple."

Nandi then transformed himself into a half-human and half-bull to serve Lord Shiva. He is the guardian and vehicle of Lord Shiva, and devotees pray to him for permission to visit Lord Shiva. He is considered the head of the Ganas of Lord Shiva and is his eternal companion.

9

The Monkey Show

"A very good astrologer has come to Ayodhya today."

These words spread like wildfire in Ayodhya, and hundreds of people flocked to different street junctures to consult this new astrologer. Reading horoscopes as well as the lines on palms was child's play for this astrologer. But his goal was different.

He was actually a thief in disguise who had come to steal something valuable. He advanced cautiously towards his goal. As soon as he reached his destination, he slowed down and relaxed. The royal palace of Ayodhya was his destination, and he attempted to steal a glance at the royal treasure.

The astrologer in disguise was none other than Lord Shiva, who was desperate to steal a glance at Lord Rama—a child in the palace of Ayodhya. When Kaushalya, Lord Rama's mother, heard about the brilliance of this astrologer, she sent a request for an audience with him. He immediately agreed and made sure he didn't show any undue excitement.

He was ushered respectfully across the royal threshold where Mother Kaushalya was eagerly waiting with her lovely son, Rama. His heart skipped a beat when Lord Shiva saw the Lord in such a lovable form. What happened next was something that disturbed Lord Shiva deeply. It was the total failure of his entire plan.

Mother Kaushalya gently nudged Lord Rama and the little child sweetly walked up to the divine astrologer, bent down gracefully and deftly touched his feet. Lord Shiva became numb! He was flabbergasted. He was embarrassed that Lord Rama had actually touched his feet.

What transpired after that in Ayodhya was all a haze. There was a great noise going on in his head. He could hear nothing of what people said to him, nor could he focus on anything that happened there. Lord Shiva found it difficult to reconcile with what had happened.

A few hours later, as he walked out of the precincts of Ayodhya, he wondered how he could undo the events of that day in his life. That's when an interesting idea struck him. That very instant, he disappeared from Ayodhya in the north and appeared thousands of *yojana* away in Anjanadri, down south.

Descending Mount Anjanadri, Lord Shiva contemplated his decision. The only way he could counteract the embarrassment he experienced at Lord Rama touching his feet was by rendering some menial service to him. And the only way Lord Rama would accept menial service as an act of repentance from Lord Shiva was if he served him through his partial incarnation. That's precisely why he had decided to come there. Here resided an expansion of Lord Shiva in the form of Hanuman.

It wasn't very difficult for him to convince the already eager Hanuman and his enthusiastic mother Anjana to take Hanuman with him to Ayodhya to visit Lord Rama. As Lord Shiva returned with Hanuman to Ayodhya, he devised a better plan this time—a plan that couldn't possibly lead to any further embarrassment. Soon a monkey-trainer entered the land of Ayodhya with his very agile monkey, who was dramatic and acrobatic.

Hearing the drumbeats of the monkey trainer, hundreds of citizens of Ayodhya flocked to the city square to watch the performance of the dynamic monkey, the likes of which they had never seen before. In sync with the drumbeats of the monkey trainer, the monkey began his startling performance. The children of Ayodhya were spellbound, as were the adults.

After a short performance, the monkey trainer and his monkey walked away to perform elsewhere. The entire crowd followed, mesmerised. They were unable to take their eyes off the two. Both of them attracted the audience like magnets. People were discussing the fact that this monkey trainer was such an expert at playing the drums that he seemed almost as competent as Lord Shiva himself.

The children of Ayodhya were all over them, trying to get the attention of the adorable monkey. Soon, the crowd reached the royal palace. Situating themselves in a strategic spot, the trainer began playing his drum, and the monkey began dancing. Their gaze was fixed at the palace gateway.

By now, a larger crowd had thronged to watch the performance. The monkey and his master were unconcerned about who or how many were watching them. They were waiting for someone special. Finally, the breath-taking moment arrived when Lord Rama came running out of the palace along with his three brothers. King Dasharatha and his three prominent queens tagged along at a distance. Both the monkey's and his trainer's hearts skipped a beat when they saw Lord Rama for the first time. In their effort to impress Lord Rama, the two performed with renewed energy.

The drummer began to drum in a way that was humanly impossible. The rhythms from his drum mesmerised all the spectators. One couldn't help but dance. The monkey somersaulted, jumped, danced, spun, and hopped, all at the speed of the mind. Lord Rama was jumping and clapping with joy.

Lord Rama's reaction excited the two further, and they performed even better. The whole scenario reached a feverish pitch, and finally the monkey-trainer pair slowed down and brought their performance to a halt. People around them clapped, whistled, showered praises on them and offered them gold coins. The King himself came forward to reward the performance.

Just then, Lord Rama said something stunning. With a sweet voice, he said, "Father, I want to keep this monkey for myself." King Dasharatha was quite embarrassed by this childish request. But the monkey trainer and his monkey were visibly thrilled. The trainer lifted the monkey in his hands and gently placed him in the loving arms of Lord Rama.

As the monkey landed in Lord Rama's arms, he closed his eyes to savour the experience of the first touch of his master. The divine touch thrilled him, and every hair on his body stood in ecstasy. Lord Rama embraced him tightly to his bosom, tears welling up in his eyes. He had reached his destination.

Everyone's attention was drawn to the unusual scene of their beloved Rama holding a monkey so dearly. King Dasharatha wanted to reward the monkey-trainer for selflessly giving away his monkey. As he turned to look at him, he couldn't find him. He looked around. All the citizens tried to locate him. It seemed that he had disappeared into thin air. Was it so? Not really, for he remained in Ayodhya in the form of his expansion—the divine monkey.

10

Mallikarjuna

Ganesha was excited to hear that Narada muni was visiting them at their home in Kailash. The son of Shiva admired Narada muni most for his intense ability to speak and entertain. Words of wisdom gushed from his mouth like a rippling waterfall. Ganesha felt refreshingly energised bathing in his profound wisdom.

Just then Narada muni entered the gate beaming from ear to ear. With his veena in his hands, he travelled across the universe, swaying to the musical glories of Lord Vishnu. He always surprised people by dropping in unannounced.

Today, he was at Kailash, but for a purpose. Of course, he loved meeting this family even without a purpose. Shiva, the topmost Vaishnava, Parvati, his devoted wife, and their two children, Ganesha and Kartikeya. Indeed, it was a special family. And he was there to give them a special gift.

As soon as they had all greeted one another lovingly, the family looked at him expectantly. His arrival meant he would share some news with them from far and wide, of demons and demigods, of love and hate, of blessings and curses. He was, after all, the first journalist ever.

Basking in their attention, Narada tossed his curly locks and began to speak. "So happy to meet all of you! I have a wonderful gift in my possession. A divine fruit. As soon as I obtained this, I wanted to give it to Ganesha and Kartikeya. They are most deserving."

Ganesha and Kartikeya were all ears at the mention of their names. It was wonderful to hear the divine sage praise them!. They looked at their parents, who were bursting with joy, and their parents nodded with pride.

Narada paused, looked at each one of them, adding more suspense to the story. And then, dramatically, he took a mango out of his bag for them to see. Ganesha, who is always eager to eat, inched closer to Narada muni in anticipation of grabbing the fruit. Meanwhile, Kartikeya, realising Ganesha's desire, stood next to Ganesha for an equal opportunity. Both of them were ready to take the mango.

Narada explained to them how special the mango was.

"This mango," he said, pointing to it as he held it up like a trophy, "is not an ordinary mango!"

The children hung onto each word he spoke. Shiva was also curious about what was so special about this particular mango.

"It contains the nectar of wisdom that even sages may not have access to. The mango juice will instantly make the recipient scholarly and wise. He will become an expert in logic and discriminative thinking. He will be a fountainhead of knowledge. But alas, I can give this mango only to one person. It cannot be shared."

Now Shiva and Parvati were in a dilemma. One fruit and two boys. How could they show any partiality? They loved them both equally. As Shiva was thinking about the problem at hand, Ganesha and Kartikeya had gone into a friendly banter, pushing each other to claim the fruit.

The parents looked at each other, exchanged a knowing glance, and then nodded in affirmation. They had found a solution. There was only one way out, and Parvati signalled to her husband to go ahead with it.

Shiva gave his decision to the excited children.

"Since both my children are extremely dear to me, let them decide who will eat the mango by having a competition."

Ganesha's heart sank. He hated competitions.

Shiva continued, "Whoever goes around the world three times first will be considered deserving to claim the fruit."

Kartikeya suppressed his mirth at the scope of the competition. He had a peacock, while Ganesha rode a mouse. No prizes for guessing who the winner would be. He immediately mounted his vehicle and shot off, confident of emerging victorious. The mango, after all, would be his.

The depth of Ganesha's despondency matched Kartikeya's buoyancy. There was no point in even trying. And then he started thinking. His father's condition was that he should circumambulate the world three times. Now which world? There was no mention of what he meant by the world.

Pleased by his logic and the solution it provided, his eyes gleamed. He smiled at his mother, Parvati, who was feeling sad at his plight. Folding his hands in reverence, Ganesha bowed down at his parents' feet and circumambulated them three times.

Surprised at his behaviour, Parvati asked him, "Dear Ganesha, why are you doing this? Don't you want to at least try? Why do you give up so easily?"

'My sweet mother, I am doing exactly what father asked me to do. My universe is my parents. There's nothing more to me than my parents. You both are my world. And I have circumambulated my world thrice. By circumambulating you, I have circumambulated the world."

Shiva and Parvati were amazed at his logic. Naturally, they could not find fault in his reasoning, and they unanimously declared him the winner. They blessed him and awarded him the mango.

The practice of circumambulating the deities originates with Ganesha. Devotees circumambulate deities, implying that God is the centre of their world and their existence.

But that was not the end. When Kartikeya returned, confident of his triumph, he was shocked to see Ganesha already enjoying the mango. He demanded to know what was going on. Learning about Ganesha's reasoning and his parents' hasty decision, he felt terribly let down. It was rather unfair to declare Ganesha the winner based on his warped logic. The terms had been spelled out clearly and he had won fair and square.

Unable to hide his pain, he declared he was going to leave home to acquire supreme wisdom through meditation. Shiva was flabbergasted by Kartikeya's unreasonable desire. No matter how much he and Parvati tried to dissuade him, he did not budge. Kartikeya left to meditate on Mount Karunch.

Unable to bear being separated, Shiva and Parvati together went there to fetch him. They pleaded and cajoled, but Kartikeya was in no mood to relent.

Not wanting to even be in their presence, Kartikeya went to another mountain to continue his meditation. Shiva and Parvati used soothing words to pacify him. They called him 'Palam nee,' which meant he was a fruit for them. As a result of being called 'Palam nee' the mountain on which Kartikeya meditated, came to be known as Palani.

Eventually, Shiva assumed the form of a Jyotirlingam because they stayed there whenever they visited Kartikeya on the mountain. This Jyotirlingam is called Mallikarjuna. Arjuna is another name for Shiva, while Mallika is Parvati. Thus, this lingam has the presence of both Shiva and Parvati. It is believed that seeing just the tip of the mountain is enough to free one from all anxieties and sins.

Shiva visits the mountain every Amavasya (New Moon Day) and Parvati visits it every Purnima (Full Moon Day). The Jyotirlingam blesses all visitors by fulfilling their desires.

Hiranyakashipu in the *Satya* yuga, Sri Rama and Sita in the *Treta* yuga, the Pandavas in the *Dwapara* yuga, and Adi Shankaracharya in the *Kali* yuga, have all visited this temple, located on the scenic banks of the River Krishna in Srisailam.

11

The Unusual Child of
Shiva and Vishnu

Mahishi was one smart buffalo-headed demon. She had turned her brother's death into an opportunity. Mahishasura, her brother, a powerful buffalo demon himself, had been demolished by Durga. But once upon a time, he had been invincible by the dint of his austerities. He stood on one leg, meditating on Brahma, consuming neither food nor water. He continued even when anthills covered his gigantic form and creepers layered on top.

The heat from his penance burst into flames and foul-smelling smoke filled the air. Finally, a pleased Brahma made his appearance to grant him a boon. What the cunning Mahishasura asked for was near-immortality. Because the boon he wanted was that he would only die at the hands of a woman, confident that no woman was powerful enough to overpower him. However, Durga shattered his illusions and put an end to his tyrannical acts.

Mahishi was extremely upset with the demise of her brother. Revenge was on her mind when she took this as an opportunity to follow in her brother's footsteps and attain mystical powers. Her brother had somehow miscalculated the power of women, but she would not. She cooked up the bizarre condition that only a child born to Shiva and Vishnu could have the potential to kill her. Brahma, however, knew her intentions, but he went on to grant her the boon. Satisfied with the immunity she had for herself, she set out to conquer the world to avenge her brother's death.

While Mahishi was engrossed in the ups and downs of her life, the world of devas and asuras was at loggerheads. Devas had lost all their powers thanks to a curse, and were in the grip of demonic evil forces. Thrown out of the heavenly planets, they had no shelter. Brahma advised them to regain their lost vigour by consuming *amrit*, the nectar obtained from churning the milky ocean, Kshirsagar. But they were so depleted that they did not even have the strength to churn the ocean.

Indra went to Vaikunta to ask Vishnu for help. Vishnu gave them unusual advice. He suggested that they join hands with the demons and make the churning of the ocean a joint project. Without their help, the weakened devas had no chance of getting the nectar.

Feeling helpless, Indra agreed. Getting the demons to embark on a joint venture with their enemies was an uphill task. It was tough to convince the demons that the devas had no hidden agenda and were willing to share the nectar with them. After much deliberation, Bali, the king of demons finally agreed to the unique proposal and the churning began.

Mount Mandar was employed as the churning rod, while Vishnu appeared as a colossal tortoise to keep the mountain base stable. Vasuki, the serpent, was the churning rope held by the demons at one end and the devas at the other. They churned the ocean for many, many years till the ocean started throwing up valuable gifts. The gifts were quickly divided between the participants.

Last to emerge was a youthful rishi, Dhanavantri, the founder of Ayurveda. His red eyes dazzled against his bluish-hued skin, clad in yellow garments. When he extended his hand-held chalice, brimming with nectar, a collective gasp echoed in the air. Before the devas could come to their senses, the greedy demons had already reached the divine youth and grabbed the chalice from his hands. A war erupted amongst the demons as each one prevented the other from sipping the nectar.

Vishnu quickly appeared in the form of an enchantress, Mohini, to distract the demons from the nectar. Mohini's voluptuous body, draped in silk and sparkling with jewels was all it took to grab their attention.

She seduced the asuras with the rhythmic movement of her sinuous limbs, and soon the mesmerised demons, handed the nectar to her, trusting her completely to share their bounty. Mohini then distributed the nectar among the devas while the bewitched asuras watched. Having regained their strength, the devas defeated the demons bringing back harmony to the world.

Word of the beautiful form of Vishnu spread far and wide, reaching the ears of Shiva. Narada muni had reached Kailash to extol the beauty of the damsel Mohini. He described her exquisite beauty in many ways. At first, Shiva dismissed Narada muni's words as exaggerated imagination.

But as Narada muni went on and on about her wonderful qualities, Shiva became impatient to see Mohini for himself.

He headed eagerly towards Mohini, and when he saw her, he was completely bowled over by her feminine oomph.

Overcome by passion, he watched her slowly advance towards him. Bees danced around them as if drunk on their passion. Teasing Shiva with her glances and smiles, Mohini led him inside the forest. Shiva followed excitedly and tried to hold her hand and embrace her. Her form was so seductive that even Shiva lost his control. Their union resulted in the birth of Shastha, from the union of Hara and Hari. Therefore, he is also known as Hariharputra.

What Mahishi had thought was impossible to achieve was not impossible after all. Shiva and Vishnu had a child, and he was known as Lord Shastha. Till then, there had been no stopping Mahishi, who was at the peak of her power, tormenting the devas and driving them out of heaven. But with the advent of Shastha, her existence was in danger.

Shastha launched an attack on the demon army. The demons retaliated and a savage battle ensued. When the dust settled down, Mahishi was horrified to see the battlefield strewn with the dead bodies of her soldiers. Mahishi had no option but to continue the fight irrespective of the outcome. When she came face to face with Shastha, he struck her down with his mace and killed her with his sword.

The jubilant devas once again recovered their kingdom and thanked Lord Shiva, Lord Vishnu, and Lord Shastha profusely for being their saviours.

12

Gangadharana

King Bhagiratha was on 'mission impossible'. A mission his ancestors had failed at. A descendent of Emperor Sagara from the Solar Dynasty, the ruler of Ayodhya, King Bhagiratha, was trying to invoke Lord Shiva in order to obtain liberation for his ancestors who had been cursed by Sage Kapila.

Extraordinary goals require extraordinary efforts. Bhagiratha was determined to do whatever it took for the welfare of his honourable ancestors. Even if it meant unprecedented austerities.

Imagine meditating while surrounded on all sides by fire and eating once a month! And imagine doing this not for a week or a month but for thousands and thousands of years. This enormous effort is famously known as *Bhagiratha Prayatnam* which has become a symbol of perseverance to achieve a goal.

Such intense austerities would have pleased any compassionate soul, and they certainly pleased Brahma. Although Brahma did appear and grant Bhagiratha's wish for the liberation of his ancestors, the matter was more complex than that. He further advised Bhagiratha to seek the blue-throated Shiva for assistance.

Not one to give up hope, Bhagiratha continued his austerities to please Lord Shiva this time. Without food and without water. Shiva, too, was touched by his unflinching devotion and appeared before him to know what was in Bhagiratha's heart.

This was the moment Bhagiratha had been waiting for. Not only Bhagiratha, but the entire Ikshvaku clan was praying for a miraculous resolution to their problems. The king began his story.

"O' Neelkanta, my story begins with my ancestor King Sagara who wanted to perform the Ashwamedha yagya to be declared the supreme king. As per the ritual, he sent a horse to traverse far and wide, inviting anyone to challenge his claim. As expected, no king wanted to challenge King Sagara.

However, when Indra heard about the yagya, he felt his throne shake. Would King Sagara challenge his supremacy too? Not wanting to risk his own throne, Indra planned to stop the yagya, and he did this by kidnapping the horse. If the horse went missing, the yagya would have to be abandoned."

Shiva listened to Bhagiratha's saga with great interest. Bhagiratha continued to be enthused by Shiva's unbridled attention.

"Indra stalked the horse and seizing the right moment, he stole it! Once he had stolen the horse, he wondered what to do with it. If the horse was found in heaven, he would be caught red-handed and Sagara would take his horse back, leaving him red-faced. So, he cleverly decided to leave the horse somewhere else. The ideal place, he thought was Sage Kapila's ashram, which was visible from where he was. The sage was immersed in meditation, so Indra quietly tied the horse in his backyard and slipped away unnoticed."

Bhagiratha paused to ensure Shiva was listening.

"When the horse went missing, Sagara sent his sixty thousand sons to find it. The agitated sons found the horse in Sage Kapila's ashram. Seeing red, they assumed the sage had stolen the horse.

Had they pondered for a moment, they would have questioned why a sage would steal a horse that was of no use to him. But they blundered and, using unpalatable words, they accused the sage of theft. The sage, for his part, glared at them furiously and, with his yogic power alone, reduced all sixty thousand princes to ashes.

The news reached King Sagara, and he quickly sent his grandson, the pious Anshuman, to appease the sage. The soft-spoken grandson begged forgiveness from the rishi, who readily forgave his uncles after seeing his respectful and repentant demeanour. The rishi told him that if the river Ganga, who is born from Vishnu, arrives from Devaloka and flows over the ashes of his uncles, then they will surely be liberated.

Since that day, many generations of the Ikshvaku dynasty have tried to invite Ganga down but have been unsuccessful. Being part of the same dynasty, I felt compassion for my ancestors and after performing prolonged austerities, I was granted audience with Brahmadeva. But he cited helplessness in the matter and suggested I approach you."

Shiva could sympathise with Bhagiratha, but he did not understand how he could assist.

"How may I help you?" he inquired with genuine concern.

"If Ganga has to come to earth, her force is so great that it would cause an upheaval. It needs someone like you to cushion her descent." Bhagiratha replied with folded hands.

"So shall it be." Shiva nodded in approval.

On Bhagiratha's request, the mighty Ganga then began her descent and fell on the matted locks of Shiva in all her fury. It was *Akshaya Tritiya*, the third day of Shukla Paksha in the month of *Vaishaka* (April–May). The torrential force was enough to crush anyone less ordinary than Shiva. Ganga's power was such that she would have devastated the entire earth with her fall. However, Shiva bore the brunt of her fall and dissipated her anger as Ganga meandered through his matted locks.

On Shiva's head, she broke into many tributaries, and once she had calmed down, she continued her earthly journey following Bhagiratha.

On the way, Ganga got diverted to Sage Jahnu's hut, where her deluge irked the meditating sage.

Angered, the sage drank up all her water. A beleaguered Bhagiratha again invoked Brahma, who cajoled Jahnu to release the river. Jahnu released the water through his ears. Finally, Bhagiratha led her to his ancestors' ashes, where he bathed them in her purity, releasing their souls.

Bathing in the Ganges, even once in a lifetime, is thought to cleanse generations of sin. Ganga forever purifies and protects from all dangers. And Lord Shiva, known as Gangadharan, with his compassion, made this possible for the citizens of the earth.

Had it not been for Shiva, Ganga would have never left heaven, and earth would have been deprived of her divine purifying presence. Because Bhagiratha was instrumental in the journey, Ganga is also called Bhagirathi. And because she emerged from Sage Jahnu's ears, she is also called Jahnvi.

13

Arjuna Wins Shiva's Grace

It was only a matter of time before war broke out. The Pandavas were in exile, knowing very well that Duryodhan would not stop at that. He would be plotting further to eliminate their claim to the throne of Hastinapur. He would not give up until he was the undisputed king. Whether the Pandavas liked it or not, whether they desired it or not, war was inevitable.

Krishna, too, the eternal well-wisher of the Pandavas, was fully aware that war was on the cards, and he wanted the Pandavas to be prepared for full-throttle combat. Fearing the worst-case scenario, he advised Arjuna to go to the Himalayas and do penance to please Lord Shiva and obtain his war weapon, the Pasupatastra.

This mighty weapon was believed to be the mother of all weapons in Vedic history. It did not even require a bow to be fired, it could simply be discharged by the mind, the eyes, and words. The unsaid code for its use was that it could only be deployed against the best of warriors. A battle of equals. Mahadeva had consumed Tripurasura, the triple city of asuras, with this very energy.

Arjuna, who was always eager to add celestial weapons to his armour, thus bid farewell to his brothers and embarked on his journey to the Himalayas at Krishna's instructions. He selected Mount Indrakila to meditate in peace. Many sages lived on the mountain top, where they practised quiet meditation.

Arjuna was performing penance for the one and only Pasupatastra. This news reached the alert ears of Duryodhana, the eldest Kaurava. Livid with rage, he sent a demon to destroy his concentration and prevent him from reaching his goal. Mookasura, the demon, took the shape of a wild boar and reached the tranquil mountain top in search of Arjuna. His arrival caused a storm overhead, with strong gales threatening to blow away the mountain itself. The sages were caught unaware and ran helter-skelter at the sudden change in weather.

Meanwhile, in Kailash, Shiva and Parvati heard about Arjuna's penance. Seeing Parvati's furrowed brows, Shiva asked her the cause. Parvati reasoned that it would be unwise to hand over the weapons of destruction to Arjuna without knowing his worthiness. After all, in the wrong hands, it could prove to be cataclysmic. Shiva wholeheartedly agreed with his consort Parvati and said, "Come, let us go and test his worthiness."

Shiva and Parvati disguised themselves as a hunter couple and hovered over Mount Indrakila. Arjuna had been stirred by a break in his concentration. He sensed a change in the environment, some negative energies trying to create mayhem around him. He opened his eyes to the bare minimum to decipher the cause. He saw the faint figure of an animal heading towards him.

Instinctively, he groped for his weapons for self-defence, but alas, he had not carried them with him, anticipating peaceful times of meditation from dawn to dusk amidst saintly sages.

Thankfully, he did have a few arrows, with which he quickly took aim and shot at the wild boar. Not one to miss his aim, the arrow hit its mark and wounded the boar. Even before Arjuna could exhale with relief, he saw another arrow whiz past him simultaneously to hit the boar. The boar suddenly transformed into the demon Mookasura.

Roaring loudly, he fell to the ground, causing the mountain to shudder under his weight. The hunter couple then descended on the scene. But to Arjuna's chagrin, the hunter said to Arjuna, "It was my arrow that killed the boar, so the credit goes to me."

The hunter's arrogant attitude angered Arjuna. His claim had no substance, as clearly it was Arjuna who had shot first, without doubt. But the hunter was adamant and was even preparing to attack Arjuna. Verbal duels led to physical aggression, and soon the two were locked in a battle for supremacy as the hunter's wife, Kirita, stood watching.

In the moonlight, their swords had a ghostly glitter, and the clanging of swords crashed into the peace of the serene environment. Birds and animals who were used to a tranquil atmosphere fled from the scene.

Kirit, the hunter, dodged and counterattacked Arjuna as he thrust his sword to annihilate him. Arjuna was flung into the air, and his sword flew out of his hand. Kirit, too, threw his sword away to engage in a hand-to-hand battle. Kirit dodged Arjuna's feeble attempts to knock him down and caught Arjuna's hand to flip him over. Arjuna realised that he was no match for this stout hunter. He needed divine intervention to save his body and, more importantly, to save his ego.

He rolled over to where his Shivalingam was, to pray to Lord Shiva. Chanting the mantras with all his heart, he offered a garland to the Lord. Kirita and Kirit stood there, watching Arjuna's actions with amusement. Next, Arjuna offered some flowers to the Shivalingam. But to his surprise, as soon as he placed the flowers before the Lord, the flowers disappeared. The garland had disappeared too.

Arjuna was bewildered, he had no clue where the flowers went. Was the Lord rejecting his worship? Disappointed, he looked around. Imagine his shock when he saw Kirit wearing the same garland and the very same flowers appearing magically at the hunter's feet.

He rubbed his eyes. Was he so tired that he was hallucinating? But Kirit was smiling. So was Kirita. Then the truth dawned upon him, and everything became crystal clear. He understood why he had not been able to overpower the hunter. Why the hunter was being unreasonably quarrelsome. The hunter was Lord Shiva himself in disguise, and the lady was Goddess Parvati. He immediately sprang up and fell at their feet, begging for forgiveness.

"Please forgive me, Mahadeva, for fighting with you. I never imagined it was you."

When Arjuna looked up, he saw Shiva and Parvati in front of him.

Shiva said, "Arjuna, it was a pleasure fighting with a renowned warrior like you. You are as good as your reputation. Tell me, what boon should I bestow upon you?"

Arjuna's cheeks flushed with pride and embarrassment. He asked, "I would like the Pasupatastra to fight against the Kauravas."

Shiva was happy to grant him the boon and he promised Arjuna that the astra would also be available to him in the future, even after the war. Although Arjuna achieved what he set out to do, in the following years he took a vow not to use any divine weapons in any battle because they could well destroy Mother Earth. Moreover, what was the use of the weapons when *dharma*, Krishna himself was on his side?

14

Banalingam

While ordinary men are two-armed, Banasura was somewhat different. No wonder, as he was the eldest of the hundred sons of Bali, who was the grandson of the illustrious Prahlad. Extraordinary traits ran in the family. After Bali, Bana was appointed the king of the asuras and ruled over Shonitpura.

Like his father, Bana too was inclined towards austerity and deity worship. He was a devout devotee of Lord Shiva. In his quest to gain more authority, he hit upon a plan to appease Shiva and obtain some magical powers from him. It was always an asset to have some added mystical skills, he reasoned.

Soon, he left for the Himalayas to undergo austerities that would please his worshipable Lord Shiva. Because Shiva is Ashutosha, or one who is easily pleased, he was quick to appear in front of Banasura to offer him a boon.

Delighted with his success, Banasura laid down his demands. Shiva blessed him with more wealth and more power. Then, taking a calculated risk, Banasura requested something more . . . something extremely devious.

"Dear Lord, could you please also grant me a thousand arms to hold a thousand weapons . . . this would help me easily defeat my enemies?" he asked.

And the unsuspecting Shiva obliged. Bana's risk paid off, and, in this way, he came to have not two, not four, but a thousand arms. And as he had wished, he could hold a thousand weapons in his arms and destroy entire armies in no time. Life became blissful as he turned from a peaceful, poised asura into a wild, warring one, subduing all who came his way. His power had grown so great that not only demons but also demigods feared his presence.

Shiva, oblivious to his horrific intentions, continued giving him grace, largely because Banasura used his thousand arms to play the drum when Shiva indulged in the Tandava dance. The rhythm produced by Bana's thousand arms was unmatched.

It gave Shiva great joy as he swayed to the thumping percussion. Seizing the right moment, Bana even asked a pleased Shiva to guard the gates of his city. A benevolent Shiva agreed to that too, although he was a bit irked at the demon's audacity.

With each passing day, Banasura's atrocities grew by leaps and bounds. The more invincible he felt, the crueller he became. He began to lose interest in it after conquering enough lands and slaying enough people. . Boredom crept in as there were no challenges left. No one could face his onslaught for more than a few minutes. The fight would end even before it began, taking away the joy of a good fight. No one could equal him in his superlative capacities.

Once again, he turned towards Lord Shiva to address his grievances.

"Dear Lord, my valour and strength are so great that no one can put up a fight with me. My thousand arms can frighten the best of seasoned warriors. But now I yearn for a decent fight and these arms have become a burden. Not able to sit quietly, my arms itch for someone to thrash, and not finding anyone, I go to the mountains and beat the mountains to pieces. Is there no one who can give me a tough fight?"

Shiva sensed that Banasura was exploding with pride. He said, "You will soon meet an opponent who will not only be your match but will also exceed your power and shatter your pride."

Banasura was excited to hear that there was someone who could actually fight him out, and in the rush of excitement, the second half of Shiva's prophecy failed to capture his attention.

The wheel of time kept moving, and Banasura got caught up in domestic problems at home. He had a young, beautiful daughter, Usha, whom he was very possessive of. She had a dream one night about a handsome prince who came and stole her heart.

So real was the dream that when she woke up, she was madly in love with the prince. She planned to elope with him because her dominating father would never allow her to fulfil her desires. She wove fantasies of her love-filled relationship and marriage with the handsome prince. But the problem was that the prince was non-existent. How could she marry him?

She confided in her friend Chitralekha about her dark secret. Chitralekha could solve any problem within minutes with her resourceful intelligence. Surely, she would know what to do. As soon as Chitralekha arrived, Usha poured her heart out to her. How she pined for the lovely prince who had the kindest of eyes and the most gorgeous smile! She swooned as she remembered his electric presence and spoke at great length about her prince charming!

Chitralekha was convinced that her friend was suffering from a bad case of lovesickness and needed to be attended to. The first step for her was to identify Usha's Prince Charming. She drew up a list of all the eligible bachelors and gods who could possibly steal her heart. Then, one by one, she drew their portraits for Usha to identify. She drew Indra, Brahma, Kartikeya, and many others. But Usha kept rejecting them all. None of them were her Prince Charming.

Lady Luck finally smiled at the two girls when Chitralekha drew the picture of Krishna's grandson, Aniruddha. Usha's face lit up, and she smiled at Chitralekha, confirming he was the one who had paid her a visit.

Now Chitralekha was not just a resourceful artist. She was also skilled in magical chants. At midnight, she used her supernatural powers to abduct Aniruddha from his castle and then transport him to Usha's private chambers.

The next morning, when Aniruddha woke up, imagine his surprise when he found himself mystically outside of Dwarka in strange surroundings! His sight fell on Usha, and he was instantly bowled over by her flawless beauty. Their eyes locked, and for Aniruddha too, it was love at first sight. Usha was already ahead in the game. To her ecstasy, he jumped out of bed and directly proposed to her. No prizes for guessing, Usha accepted his hand and proposal.

Now it was time for the real test. When Banasura heard of the love story unfolding in his daughter's life, he roared like an injured tiger. Who dared to woo his daughter? He instructed his army to imprison his daughter in a fortress surrounded by fire and kill Aniruddha. Aniruddha showed his mettle by defeating the army. Then Banasura himself came to fight with Aniruddha, and with his serpentine arms granted by Shiva, he captured Aniruddha and imprisoned him too.

The news of Aniruddha's kidnapping and affair with Banasura was delivered to Krishna by the ever-present Narada muni. Krishna naturally rounded up his huge army and reached Shonitpura firing on all cylinders. Balarama, Satyaki, Pradyumna, and other stalwarts led the army to surround the enemy camp. Banasura was initially ecstatic about the prospect of fighting someone of his calibre. But his excitement turned into dismay when he fought with all his might and yet his powers and skills were petty in front of Sri Krishna.

Krishna could easily counter all his moves and perhaps even better them. When realisation dawned on him that he would not be able to defeat Krishna, he once again turned to Lord Shiva for help, his saviour in all crises. But alas, no matter how much he prayed to him, Shiva did not arrive. Krishna was on a rampage. His Sudarshan Chakra was in action, chopping off the arms of Banasura. One by one, the Sudarshan Chakra went 'whizz' then 'craaackk' and then there was a 'thudd' with the falling of arms.

The air echoed with 'whizz!' 'craaackk!' 'thudd!' Shiva's prophecy was coming true. That Banasura would soon encounter someone with superior combat skills and decapitate his pride. When the Sudarshan Chakra was down to the last pair of arms, Banasura again called out to Shiva. This time, Shiva appeared to protect his devotee. He requested Krishna to spare Banasura and two of his arms, as he had learnt his lesson. On Shiva's appeal, Krishna recalled his Chakra and acceded to his wish, sparing the humbled demon.

Banasura's downfall meant Usha could tie the knot with Aniruddha without any hurdles. Krishna blessed the union, and the procession returned to Dwarka with the joyful couple.

Meanwhile, Banasura had turned introspective and sat on the banks of the River Narmada, reflecting. He meditated on Lord Shiva for directions. He had seen and done all. He had lived a life larger than life, which perhaps no one in the universe could imagine. Living with a thousand arms had given him supreme powers and some out-of-the-box experiences. But he had never felt at peace. Now he was ready for something that was more satisfying. Maybe Shiva could guide him with that too.

When Shiva appeared, he humbly expressed his desire to become one of his ganas. He also asked for his Shivalingam to be known as Bana Lingam so that people would remember his story. Shiva blessed him with all that he desired.

The Bana Lingams discovered in Narmada are thought to be the forms of Shiva that Shiva took in order to fulfil Banasura's request. They are said to be Svayambhu Lingams as they are untouched by human hands. Shaligrams are for Vishnu and Bana Lingams are for Shiva. They are self-manifested representations. The Narmada itself sprang from the body of Lord Shiva and is also called Shankari, or daughter of Lord Shiva.

Bana Lingam belongs to the family of five stones called *Panchayatana*. Five Hindu deities are considered to be embodiments of the five bhutas/tattvas, which are worshipped as formless stones found in five different rivers in India. Each divine stone represents a different deity and is placed on the sacred altar in preparation for Panchayatana worship.

Deity	Bhuta (tatva)	Stone	River
Vishnu	Earth	Shaligrams	Gandaki (Nepal)
Shiva	Water	Bana Lingam	Narmada (Madhya Pradesh)
Ganesha	Space	Sonabhadra	Sone (Bihar)
Indra	Air	Swarnamukhi	Swarnamukhi (Andhra Pradesh)

15

Son of Ocean

This Puranic story is about a boy who grows up to become the king of demons. What is remarkable about him is not that he became demon king, but that he had many divine connections and yet fate had a demonic life planned for him. And though he led a demonic lifestyle, eventually he met a divine death at the hands of Lord Shiva.

The unusual events unfolded one day when Indra, king of *Devaloka*, accompanied by Brihaspati, *guru* of the devas, was on his way to Kailash to meet Lord Shiva. Lord Shiva decided to test their attitude and sat in their way, disguised as a *yogi*, blocking them from going ahead. Indra failed to recognise Shiva and haughtily instructed the yogi to move out of the way.

The yogi pretended not to hear him, arousing Indra's wrath. Irked by the indifference displayed by the yogi, Indra threatened to use his thunderbolt. Shiva waited to see what Indra would do next, expecting him to realise at any moment that the yogi was Shiva himself. However, anger is blinding, and Indra was so consumed by it that instead of pausing and reflecting on the unconventional behaviour of the yogi, he actually removed his deadly thunderbolt to strike Lord Shiva himself. Indra's intolerance displeased Shiva greatly, causing his third eye to open. The opening of the third eye could only mean inauspiciousness or disaster. Indra's arm got paralysed in mid-air, and his thunderbolt was rendered useless. He got the fright of his life to see the yogi's eyes blazing red with rage.

Brihaspati did not pause to understand that they had encountered not just any ordinary person but Lord Shiva himself. The very person whose audience they were seeking. Brihaspati also knew that Shiva's rage could very well destroy Indra. Taking control of the situation, he intervened to beg Shiva to forgive Indra. Indra too, jolted out of his arrogance, joined Brihaspati in asking forgiveness for his violent action.

Shiva simmered down, but the fire in his third eye could not be ignored. It needed a target to fire at. Shiva immediately turned his glance avoiding directing his vision at Indra. That would have been catastrophic for Indra, burning him to ashes. He turned towards Gangasagar, the meeting of the Ganga with the ocean. And the fiery ball merged with the water, transforming into a baby boy.

The infant was an intense bundle of energy, crying ferociously and screaming his lungs out. The ocean god came out, startled to find the cause behind the ruckus. Seeing the baby, he wondered how and from where he had arrived at his door. The child's shrieking pierced through the air, deafening even the sages and demigods. All of them turned to Lord Brahma to help them find a solution.

Lord Brahma arrived and was pleasantly surprised to see the hyperactive baby. The ocean waves put the child in his lap as he tried to pacify him by fondling him in his arms. But the dynamite baby did not like the intrusion, and he pressed Brahma's neck with such aggression that Brahma lost his balance. Unable to bear the pain, Brahma put the aggressive child down.

The ocean god asked Brahma about the child's name and future. The all -knowing Brahma replied, "This child will be called Jalandhar and is the future king of asuras. His power is such that no one can kill him except Lord Shiva."

The ocean was mighty impressed and took the child home. Jalandhar grew up under the care of the ocean god with great love and affection. Time passed quickly, and he was soon married to Vrinda, daughter of the demon Kalanemi. As predicted by Brahma, Jalandhar eventually became the king of demons. He was loved by his fellow demons for his strength and nobility. He was a fair and just king.

One day he had a visitor—the exalted Sage Bhrigu. He told Jalandhar the history of demons like Hiranyakashipu and Virochana. He narrated the interesting saga of the churning of the ocean to generate many valuable gifts.

This particular story evoked a lot of curiosity from Jalandhar because it was about his own father. It incensed him infinitely to know that his father had literally been looted by the devas for their own selfish reasons. And as the sage told him more details, his fury only increased hearing how his father gave up so many precious possessions—Kamadhenu, the cow of plenty; Airavat, the four-tusked-elephant now with Indra; Uchchaihshravas, the celestial horse; Chandra, the moon; and Parijat, a fragrant plant now in heaven.

The list was endless, and Jalandhar cringed as the sage continued to tell him how all the treasures were distributed amongst asuras and devas.

All of these should have been his because he was the rightful owner as the son of the ocean god. Jalandhar's mind began to plot how he would recover his lost bounty. He decided to play it straight by sending a messenger to the king of the heavens, Indra asking for his belongings back. If Indra had any sense, he would understand the wrongs he had done and return everything without a fuss.

Jalandhar's messenger left and soon returned empty-handed. Indra had simply laughed in his face and driven him out of his kingdom. Indra had succeeded in adding salt to Jalandhar's injury with this act. Roaring madly with pain and insult, Jalandhar attacked the heavens with his army in full force, leaving no scope for the devas to put up any resistance. They fled their abodes, unable to face the demonic onslaught.

The devas had no option but to take shelter with Lord Vishnu. Usually, Vishnu heard their grievances and annihilated the demons. But this time, he was in a fix. He could not commit to killing Jalandhar because his consort, Lakshmi, considered Jalandhar her brother. They both belonged to the ocean. Both were raised in the loving lap of the ocean god. She did not want Jalandhar to be killed. And he gave her his assurance that he would not be.

Nonetheless, Vishnu left to teach Jalandhar a lesson. It was a fierce battle that was about to end with Vishnu beheading the demon with his sword, but Lakshmi intervened at the nick of time and stopped Vishnu from doing it.

Vishnu then informed Jalandhar about Lakshmi's protection for him and even gave him a boon as a reward for the good fight. Jalandhar requested that Vishnu allow him to take up residence in Kshirsagar along with Lakshmi. Vishnu obliged and with this move, Jalandhar became the ruler of all three worlds, hell, heaven, and earth. The devas, on the other hand, were dissatisfied because they remained homeless. Narada muni came to their rescue and offered to do something for them.

Narada had a very simple methodology that always worked when it came to dealing with demons. He knew their psychology a bit too well. He arrived at Jalandhar's palace and executed his plan. During their conversation, Narada muni casually mentioned how beautiful Kailash was and how no other place could match it. . Jalandhar became green with envy and boasted how beautiful his own palace and kingdom were. Narada muni had expected this kind of answer and he played his next shot. He said even if he had a more palatial and scenic environment than Kailash, he still didn't have an enchanting consort like Goddess Parvati. This jolted Jalandhar out of his comfort zone and taking advantage of his silence, Narada muni extolled how virtuous and ravishing she was in numerous ways.

Jalandhar's competitive mind, of course, could not bear others having something that he did not. He instantly decided to send a messenger to Kailash. Rahu, his messenger, gave Shiva the message that, since he was an ascetic, having a consort was extremely hypocritical of him. He should immediately hand over Parvati to Jalandhar or face dire consequences.

The threatening message made Shiva see red and a creature called Kirtimukha, sprang up from his brows. This ferocious creature nearly killed Rahu, who ran for his life. Jalandhar then prepared for war and launched an attack on the Himalayan abode Kailash.

However, he found only Nandi there because Shiva and Parvati had moved to a mountain near Lake Manasa. Nandi and the other demigods fought valiantly but they were not as powerful as Jalandhar and his army. Finding Nandi on the losing side of the battle, Shiva had to jump into the battlefield himself. Before leaving, he urged Parvati to be careful because he suspected the asuras might come for her disguised as well-wishers.

Jalandhar knew it would be difficult to defeat Shiva and his army, so he resorted to trickery. He created the illusion of apsaras to distract the enemies. While the beautiful apsaras danced and sang to entertain Shiva's army and keep them in a trance, Jalandhar himself assumed the appearance of Shiva and went to meet Parvati. But Parvati was fully alert and recognised the deceit. In anger, her eyes turned red and her skin turned black as she transformed herself into Kali to avenge Jalandhar's deception. The fearsome transformation was so menacing that Jalandhar quickly made his escape, lest he lose his life at the hands of Parvati.

Shaken up by the ordeal, Parvati went to meet Vishnu. She wanted tit for tat. In a fit of anger, she suggested that Vishnu too should disguise himself as Jalandhar and woo his wife, Vrinda. Vrinda was a very pious woman and losing her chastity surely meant death for her. Vishnu agreed and planned a rendezvous with Vrinda, disguised as Jalandhar.

Vrinda was only too happy to believe that her husband had returned unscathed from the war and hugged him tight. Vishnu spent many blissful days with her. But one day, Vrinda realised that Vishnu had tricked her. Embarrassed and humiliated, she wanted to end her life. But before giving up her life, she cursed Vishnu, saying that he too would have a similar fate and experience his wife's abduction and separation from her.

This curse eventually took effect in the *Ramayana* when Vishnu's avatar Rama's wife Sita was abducted by Ravana. Immediately after cursing Vishnu, Vrinda self-immolated by jumping into a fire.

Jalandhar heard the news and renewed the battle with Shiva. He wanted to destroy everyone for the grief he was suffering. Shiva decided to end the game of life for Jalandhar once and for all. He thrust his *trishul* into his chest, and using his toe to create a *chakra*, he beheaded Jalandhar. Jalandhar, by virtue of being killed by Lord Shiva, achieved liberation.

16

Ravana Covets Kailash

L earned yet arrogant. Handsome yet cold-hearted. Devout yet selfish. These were the dichotomous characteristics of Ravana, the king of Lanka. His knowledge, his heroism, and his worship were all in vain because he was proud beyond measure, unbelievably narcissistic, and his cruelty had no end. He even believed that he was superior to all, simply by virtue of his birth.

One day he decided to gift Lord Shiva's Atmalingam to his mother. This would make her worship a lot easier. This endeavour entailed traveling a long distance, all the way from Lanka to the mighty Himalayas, where Lord Shiva resided. But he resorted to doing anything for his mother.

Once he reached the scenic foothills of Mount Kailash, he readied himself for an arduous spell of austerities to please Mahadeva. Nothing could be obtained without pleasing him. Ravana also knew that Shiva had a soft corner for him and he would never deny him anything he asked for.

With this faith, he bathed in the lotus-filled pools with sparkling water and energised himself to follow the preliminary rituals of prayers to Agni, Surya, and others. Soon, he was deeply immersed in his meditation on Lord Shiva, chanting his names with fierce determination. But this time, Shiva did not respond immediately. He waited for more. Year after year, Ravana kept up the penance and austerities to attract Bholenath.

After a prolonged period of meditation that went on longer than he had expected, Ravana began to lose patience. Desperate for Shiva's attention, he thought of doing something radical. What could be more radical than chopping off his heads and presenting them to his deity?

One by one, he started chopping off his heads as a sacrifice. This was such an unprecedented sacrifice that it generated energy enough to burn all of creation. It was at its peak when he chopped the ninth head, causing all snow-clad peaks to lose their ice and glaciers to melt.

There was intense heat and flooding of water masses at the same time. And just as Ravana was about to sever his tenth and last head, the heat suddenly cooled off as if a switch had been flipped. The cool breeze kissed the green velvet mountains, giving the world a pleasant respite. The sudden change in atmosphere only meant that Lord Shiva had arrived, pleased with the suicidal sacrifices of Ravana.

He said, "Ravana, you have pleased me with your self-effacing austerity. Tell me what boon can I give you?"

Overjoyed with the success of his strategy, he revealed the purpose of his penance.

"O Lord, please give me your Atmalingam for my venerable mother to worship.". I have come only for that."

It was an unusual request, but Shiva had promised to fulfil it and reluctantly handed over the Atmalingam. He cautioned Ravana to hold it in his hand all the way to Lanka. If he ever put it down, it would be firmly planted and would remain there indefinitely.

Ravana held on to his precious possession, determined to carry it all the way to Lanka. Little did he know that there were other forces working against him to make his 'Project Atmalingam' a flop show.

The demigods were keen that the powerful Atmalingam should not be carried to Lanka, lest it would make Ravana more powerful and arrogant. That would spell a large-scale disaster for the devas. They asked Lord Ganesha to help solve their problem; he thought over the issue and came up with a wise plan. Assuming the guise of a cowherd boy, he made himself visible around Ravana at dusk.

Dusk was the time when Ravana did his daily evening prayer rituals, without missing even a single day. While carrying the Atmalingam, Ravana was a tad worried. How would he perform the prayer that day? His hands were holding his trophy and he could not put it down. But as he sighted the cowherd boy, a crooked smile appeared on his ghastly face.

He approached the boy and asked him to hold the lingam for him for a short while. The cowherd boy cunningly replied that he would do it, but only for a short while. If Ravana did not return soon, he would put it down and leave. Ravana agreed and busied himself. The cowherd boy, delighted at the easy deception, waited for a moment and then placed the lingam on the ground, setting it there for eternity. Ganesha, thus, foiled Ravana's plans allowing the devas to have their way.

To this day, the lingam exists to commemorate this victory in Deogarh. And it is worshipped as *Baidyanath* because Shiva acted as a physician or *vaidya* to heal all of Ravana's heads so that they could join his body again.

Although it was a victory for the devas, their king, Indra, was still a worried man. Ravana had enough boons and blessings from Shiva to continue to create havoc in their lives. How does one stop a tyrant blessed with divine sanction? Quite impossible, Indra thought. He was still in a pensive mood when the travelling sage Narada muni entered his kingdom. Indra poured out his troubled heart to the sympathetic muni hoping for a relief balm from him.

Narada muni heard Indra's story of how Ravana had sliced his heads to obtain the Atmalingam from Shiva and how Shiva had put a condition that it should not be placed down else it would remain lodged there forever. And how the demigods outsmarted him to hand over the lingam to Ganesha.

Yet, Indra had the lingering feeling that he was never safe from Ravana. He could attack them and defeat them any day. Narada muni agreed with him and plans began to formulate in his mind to help the helpless devas. Assuring the tormented king of his full support, he left.

He headed straight to Lanka to meet the lankan supremo Ravana. Although he had visited him multiple times before, he never failed to be impressed and magnetised by Lanka's opulence in general and Ravana's lavish palace in particular. Decorated with the most precious stones, situated on a hill top, the palatial verandas overlooked the most pristine scenery dotted with lakes and gardens.

Unexpectedly, he was warmly ushered in and taken straight to Ravana who was also in a sombre mood after losing out on the infinite power of the Atmalingam. He confided in Narada muni how he had been so close and yet so far from obtaining the precious gift.

Ravana had presented him with the perfect opportunity to unfold his plan. Delighted, he said to him, "Dear King, an opportunity lost is another opportunity to gain something more. I have a suggestion for you after hearing about your intense dedication and desire. Rather than obtaining the Atmalingam, I propose to you . . ."

And then Narada muni dramatically lowered his voice to create an ambience of secrecy. He drew closer to Ravana's ears, afraid that his plan would be revealed. Narada muni's theatrical actions convinced Ravana that the sage was his true well-wisher and was going to suggest something really special to him.

Ravana inched closer to the muni, hanging on to every word.

Having ensured that Ravana was in his trap, Narada continued, ". . . I propose that instead of being simply content with a small part, why not go for the kill?"

Hearing the word 'kill', Ravana's excitement soared. He inched closer.

"What I mean to say is that you possess unmatched strength. With your strength, you can carry not only the Atmalingam, but the entire Mount Kailash back to Lanka on your hands. Wouldn't that be wonderful? It will elevate your daily worship to a higher level."

Ravana's eyes gleamed at this radical idea. Narada muni was quite a genius, he thought. The more he thought about it, the more attractive the idea was till he could no longer wait and decided to leave right away to execute the plan and bring Mount Kailash along with Lord Shiva and Goddess Parvati to Lanka.

Even before Narada muni could take his leave, Ravana dashed and jumped onto his plane to take him to the Himalayas again. Once at Mount Kailash, he grasped the bottom of the mountain and pulled with all his strength in order to carry it back with him. His attempt led to rumbling and shaking which in turn disturbed Shiva's penance. He opened his eyes and looked enquiringly at Parvati Devi. She replied with a faint smile, "Your devotee Ravana has the audacity to believe he can uproot our abode and carry it back with him . . ."

Shiva was both amused and angry. He had never heard of anything like this. Many had come to please him and ask for boons, but none had ever tried to forcefully carry him back. He addressed Ravana, "Your arrogance has no end. It is your ego that drives you to do such insane things. Soon, a great personality will be born only to vanquish your existence."

With these words, Shiva pressed his toe against the earth pushing Mount Kailash firmly on the ground and crushing Ravana under it, catapulting him to the *Patal loka*. Ravana cried in pain at the sudden turn of events. For the next fourteen days, Ravana, in acute agony, kept chanting mantras asking for forgiveness from Shiva.

In desperation, he composed the *Shiva Tandava Stotra* hoping to appease Shiva and get his pardon. This prayer was so heartfelt and powerful that Shiva was moved upon hearing it and taking pity on Ravana, he finally released him from his distress in Patal Loka.

The Shiva Tandava Stotra is chanted with devotion even today to gain numerous benefits by pleasing Lord Shiva.

17

How Parrots Learnt to Imitate

Surely you would have heard of talking parrots . . . but have you heard of hearing parrots? One such parrot lived in Vrindavan. He was Radha's favourite parrot. She loved him dearly. Every day, she would feed him pomegranate seeds with her own loving hands. He reciprocated wonderfully. He first learnt the word that she loved the most—Krishna!

The parrot would call out Krishna's name all day, making her happy. Radha kept him perched constantly on her left hand because he kept her so happy by reminding her of Krishna all through the day.

When the Vrindavan pastimes of Radha and Krishna wounded up, Radha instructed her favourite pet parrot to remain in this world and remind everyone here about Krishna, just like he would remind her. Thus, the parrot did as told, waiting for an opportunity to hear and share stories about Krishna with the world.

But the pain of separation from Radha and Krishna was killing him and he was desperately seeking an association with someone who could remind him and help him immerse himself once again in thoughts of Krishna. He was flying all over the world looking for a reservoir of the nectar of Krishna *katha*.

As he hovered over a place known as Ekamra Kanan, he was bowled over by a voice from below.

The voice was soothing and yet so authoritative. Most importantly, that voice was constantly speaking the name Krishna, every few seconds as if compulsively drawn towards repeating that divine name. The parrot immediately descended and perched itself on a mango tree branch. That divine sound was surely emanating from under that tree.

Later, he realised that he had unknowingly landed in the most holy land of Ekamra Kanan, the holy abode of Lord Shiva and Parvati. And the person speaking the name of Krishna was none other than Lord Shiva himself. Seated next to him was Parvati, attentively listening to the narration. Bhubaneshwar was narrating the Krishna katha to Bhubaneshwari, and there was no one else in the near vicinity. During their private times together, they loved to discuss the *Bhagavatam* and help each other remember the Supreme Lord.

On arrival, the parrot heard Lord Shiva narrating a section from the first canto of *Srimad Bhagavatam* which delineates the greatness of Sri Krishna. Parvati was very eager to hear stories of Krishna directly but Shiva wasn't going to begin narrating those anytime soon. He always preferred that the audience hear the holy text right from the beginning.

The first nine cantos of *Srimad Bhagavatam* talk about the greatness of Krishna and then the tenth canto talks about the sweetness of Krishna. Shiva was so immersed in his narration that he had closed his eyes and was continuously narrating the *Bhagavatam* from his memory. Parvati would respond to the narration by making a little sounds just so that the narrator knew that she was listening attentively. "Hmm ... hmm ... hmm.", said Parvati at regular intervals.

The little parrot was loving every single detail of this narration. He hadn't got a chance to hear so many details about his worshipable master in a long time. With every new learning, he felt like dancing and singing loudly, but he kept control over himself, not wanting to disturb the flow of the narration. Parvati was really not into the philosophical understanding of the *Bhagavatam* as she preferred the exciting stories and that was what she was waiting for. Especially stories of Krishna in Vrindavan.

Every now and then there would be a story, but there were parts with heavy philosophical narration that sometimes stretched for over an hour. Those were challenging times for Parvati as she struggled to remain awake. And her husband wasn't even looking at her. He was absorbed in higher truths and his eyes remained closed to the truths of this world. And the truth was that Parvati had fallen asleep right in the middle of his narration.

The parrot above quickly perceived the emergency at hand. The sounds of Parvati had stopped totally and she was fast asleep. The parrot became terrified as he realised what was about to happen. If Shiva realised that Parvati had dozed off, he would immediately stop the narration and that would be a great loss to the parrot. After all, he had travelled far and wide to get access to such a divine narrator. Now, he couldn't afford to not hear the complete narration. The only option was for him to act without requiring Shiva to open his eyes.

Imitating the voice of Parvati, the parrot began saying, "Hmm . . . hmm . . . hmm." He imitated it to such perfection, even perfectly including the intervals at which the sounds came. Hours passed and the narration continued unabated.

Suddenly, at one point Shiva opened his eyes. He saw that Parvati was fast asleep. Yet, the sound had continued during his narration. He immediately sensed the presence of a third person who had dared to intrude into their privacy. With great anger he asked, "Who is that saying 'Hmm'? Who is hiding and listening to my narration without permission?"

Shiva got up and began peering into the tree from where the sound came. He suddenly heard the flutter of wings and out flew a parrot. With his hands raised and his fists clenched, Shiva began to run behind that flying interloper. The parrot flew with great speed hoping and praying that it could save itself from Shiva's wrath.

Flying all the way from Bhubaneshwar to Badrinath, the parrot desperately sought shelter there. While looking for a place to stay, the parrot spotted the ashram of Vedavyasa. Exactly at that moment, Vedavyasa was narrating the *Srimad Bhagavatam* to his wife. For a second, the bird perched itself on the door of the little hut and looked for a safe place to hide. Suddenly, it had a bright idea. The parrot saw that Vyasa's wife was listening to the Bhagavatam with rapt attention and her mouth wide open in amazement. Taking that opportunity, the parrot flew into her mouth and took residence in her womb. Obviously, the parrot was in its celestial form so it wasn't really a physical existence.

The parrot remained in the womb of Vyasdeva's wife for a really long period of time during which it heard the entire Bhagavatam being narrated by the great sage himself. Thus, it found the best place to stay and continue listening to the Bhagavatam.

After about sixteen years in the womb, the parrot emerged in the form of a human child. Vyas named the child Shukha, knowing very well that he was the divine form of Radha's favourite parrot of Radha. Shukhadeva went on to become the foremost narrator of Srimad Bhagavatam. While he narrated the entire Bhagavatam to Parikshit, the grandson of Arjuna, both Shiva and Vyasdeva were present. He had learnt from both of them, but when he spoke the Bhagavatam, he added such sweetness to it due to his intimate connection with Radha and Krishna in Vrindavan, that it seemed that the Bhagavatam had become more melodious.

Because he was the parrot of Radha, Shukha could never take her name during the narration of the Bhagavatam, both out of etiquette and also out of fear of being lost in ecstasy if he did. Parikshit had limited time, so Shukha restrained himself from using the name Radha throughout the narration.

18

Bhimashankar

Bhima, son of Karkati and a demon, always knew he was exceptionally strong. Demons are known to have extra strength and Bhima was no exception. But even amongst other demon boys his age, he stood out. Other boys were afraid to get into a scuffle with him because he would easily overpower them.

As he grew older, he became more and more aware of the differences between him and the others. Not only was he superior in strength but he also had a gigantic form compared to others. He towered over them like a giraffe looking down at rabbits.

Unable to solve this mystery by himself, he asked his mother one day about the secret behind his size which often caused him acute embarrassment. Karkati, his mother was aware of Bhima's awkwardness and curiosity behind it. She decided it was the right time to tell him the truth.

"Son," she said, "You are the son of Kumbhakarna, brother of Ravana, the king of Lanka. Kumbhakarna was an exceptionally huge demon, due to a boon given to him by Suryadeva. And you have taken after him, my child. You are like your father."

Bhima felt a burden lifting from his shoulders. In fact, he was reeling with so much joy, he felt giddy. He had never seen or known his father and any connection with him was extremely satisfying. His chest puffed up knowing that he was like his father. He wanted to know more about him.

"Mother, pray tell me everything about my father! What was he like? Where is he now?"

Karkati smiled sadly. She would have to tell him the whole truth now.

"Your father was a very brave and noble warrior but unfortunate as well. I met him here, in Dakini forest. I was all alone and fell in love with him. You were born as a result of our love. He then returned to Lanka.

"Thanks to a misunderstanding with Brahmadeva, he slept a lot. His brother Ravana had kidnapped Rama's wife Sita and he wanted Kumbhakarna to fight against Rama. Kumbhakarna explained to Ravana that his actions were wrong. He was the only one who understood that Rama was not a human but a divine being. But, against his own wishes, and out of loyalty to his brother, he went into the battlefield and was killed by Rama. Ravana was killed too and the youngest brother Vibhishan was crowned king of Lanka. And we continued to stay in this forest."

Bhima was remorseful to learn how his father had died. He felt anger and hatred towards his killer, Rama. Not only was his father gone, but, as his son, he was deprived of the throne too. Instead, he was living in the forest as a nobody. He was seething with rage at the injustice meted out to him. He decided to direct all his rage at Rama and vowed to take revenge.

Taking permission from his mother, he left home to commence a period of penance and austerities. His plan was to appease Lord Brahma and equip himself with supernatural powers that would then help him take revenge from his enemies and establish himself as the king of not just Lanka but the entire universe. Now that he knew his heritage, now that he knew what he was capable of, now that he knew what he deserved, he would go all out and claim it.

He stuck to his plan fastidiously for thousands of years. Without food, he survived only on water and determination until finally Brahma was involuntarily pulled towards him to bestow his blessings. When asked what he wanted, Bhima was ready with his wants.

He wanted infinite power and unlimited wealth to conquer the world. Brahma granted his wishes, leaving a euphoric and energised Bhimasura behind. Bhima thought he had finally embarked on the journey of being the Lord and the master of the universe, but in reality, he had his downfall waiting for him. No one has ever benefitted from harbouring hatred, revenge, and desire for control.

Acquiring the boons had charged him up and he went on a rampage destroying everything in his way like a mad, ruthless elephant. Soon, he had driven the celestials out of the heavenly kingdoms to take control of all worldly planets. Indra was rendered homeless and throneless. As this was not the first time Indra was in this situation, he did what he had previously done—take shelter with the generous Shiva as he always assured him of emerging victorious against the evil forces.

Meanwhile, Bhima was enjoying his success in turning the world upside down. He had captured and imprisoned King Rishabh along with his wife. King Rishabh was a gentle and spiritual soul undisturbed by the upheavals in his life. Even though in prison, he made a Shivalingam out of mud and continued his daily worship unaffected.

News reached Bhima that King Rishabh was trying to invoke Shiva and that drove him wild. How dare his prisoners worship a deity under his rule? He stormed into the prison and found the saintly couple deep in meditation in front of the Shivalingam. In a fit of manic rage, he kicked the "sinners" aside and struck down the lingam too with his legs.

This time, Bhima had gone too far crossing all limits of tolerance. The earth rumbled violently under his feet causing panic all around. From deep within emerged the glorious Lord Shiva. Even then Bhima did not come to his senses. Arrogance was so deeply ingrained in him that he thought he could conquer even divine powers. He lunged at Shiva with a loud cry, thrusting his sword at him. Shiva stopped his sword with his trident, breaking it into two.

Shiva's peaceful demeanour was now turning into agitation. His amber eyes and flaring nostrils emitted fiery sparks enough that would burn the object of his anger. Bhima had exhausted all his weapons and was now at his wit's end. He had been unsuccessful in overpowering Shiva. Shiva decided that it was time to end Bhima's reign. With his *trishul*, he pierced Bhima who collapsed on the ground in agonising pain. Soon, he breathed his last, and was liberated from the demonic body.

Lord Shiva manifested himself on that spot and is worshipped as Bhimashankar Jyotirlingam. A groove divided the lingam into two with the top part considered to be Shiva, and bottom Parvati. He is therefore depicted as Ardhanareshwar. It is believed that the Pandavas and Kauravas learnt archery from Dronacharya at this place.

19

Ekambareshwar

I n shloka 7.4 of the *Bhagavad Gita*, Lord Krishna
says

"bhūmir-āpo 'nalo vāyuḥ kham mano buddhir eva cha
ahankāra itīyam me bhinnā prakṛitir aṣhṭadhā"

Earth, water, fire, air, space, mind, intellect, and
ego—these are eight components of my material
energy.

Earth, water, fire, air, and space are the building
blocks of the material world. Life originates from a
combination of these five prime elements. These
Pancha Bhootas are said to be in the hands of Lord
Shiva, and their purpose is the destruction of the
universe.

In South India, there are five temples that represent
each element of nature and are dedicated to Lord
Shiva. As per Ayurveda, the body is in harmonious
health when the five elements are in alignment.

Four of the Pancha Bhoota Sthalas (Pancha
means five, Bhoota means elements and Sthala means
place) or the temples are in Tamil Nadu, and one is
in Andhra Pradesh, with lingams as representations
of the Pancha Bhootas. They were constructed a
thousand years ago in a geographical straight line
without the use of satellite technology, demonstrating
the incredible expertise of scholars at the time. The

alignment of the temples is such that they resonate spreading positive energy in the entire region.

Temple	Element	Location
Ekambareshwarar Temple	Earth/Prithvi	Kanchipuram
Jambukeshwarar Temple	Water/Jal	Tiruvanaikaval
Arunachaleshwara Temple	Fire/Agni	Tiruvannamalai
Kalahasti Temple	Air/Vayu	Kalahasti, Andhra Pradesh
Thillai Nataraja Temple	Space/Akash	Chidambaram

Kanchipuram is one of the seven most sacred cities in India. The Saptapuris or seven special cities are Ayodhya, Dwarka, Haridwar, Kashi, Kanchipuram, Mathura, and Ujjain. They are sacred because they have special purity as Mokshapuris, the power to liberate a soul from worldly sins to attain salvation. Amongst the seven, Kanchipuram and Kasi are the holiest. Dying in Kasi and being born in Kanchipuram assures salvation to the soul.

Situated in Kanchipuram, the temple city of India, is the Prithvi Lingam in Ekambareshwarar temple. It is made out of sand to depict the earth element.

One fine day, in spring, Lord Shiva was absorbed in meditation at Mount Kailash. Nature was at its youthful best with polychromatic flowers spreading intoxicating fragrances with the help of a gentle cooling breeze. Rainbows arched themselves to extend more colour to the skyline as bees and insects got drunk on pollen nectar. Peacocks fanned out their feathers to join the ecstasy. The earth was swaying in sync with Shiva's breathing. Overwhelmed with the festive mood around her, Parvati too felt elated and light-hearted. Letting go of her self-control, she tiptoed behind her beloved and covered his eyes jovially with her delicate hands.

Unaware to all including Parvati, Shiva was immersed in his task of universal administration. Parvati's unexpected act startled him and interrupted his flow of work. As soon as his eyes were covered, darkness descended on the world. The darkness sucked the life out of living beings because no life can sustain itself without the energy of light.

Although the disturbance was momentary on Mount Kailash, it lasted for aeons and aeons on earth. Shiva's half a moment was equivalent to millions of earthly years. This prolonged descent into darkness led to the destruction of all living beings and the dissolution of the planetary system.

The innocent, loving moment had turned into one of devastation, arousing Shiva's anger. He ended up banishing Parvati to earth in order to atone for her sin. On earth, Parvati headed for Kanchipuram, the holiest of cities. Her desire was to perform penance in Kanchipuram to appease Lord Shiva. A huge mango tree, laden with ripe mangoes and the hub for many exotic birds, caught her fancy. She sat under this tree to begin her meditation and worship.

Years rolled by and Shiva remained unmoved. Parvati too, continued her austerities uninterrupted. Her dedication finally prompted Shiva to test her sincerity. The ground where Parvati sat was suddenly surrounded by fire. Without panicking, Parvati called on Lord Vishnu for help. Vishnu simply used the moon situated on Shiva's head to cool down the fire. The cooling beams of Chandradeva when directed to the fire, caused the fire to simmer down and finally extinguish.

Unfazed, she continued her worship. She sculpted a lingam from sand to pursue meditating on Lord Shiva relentlessly. Shiva too continued testing her. He directed the River Vegavati towards Parvati's Shivalingam. The river water flooded the area, threatening to wash away her object of worship. Terrified of losing her lingam, Parvati flung herself over the lingam, protecting it with her body. She hugged the Shivalingam so that the water would flow over her. This gesture really touched Shiva's heart. After this, he did not want to test her further. He appeared in front of her and lovingly asked her to marry him again. Parvati accepted his offer, and they returned to Kailash.

Preparations were on for Shiva and Parvati's marriage, which was to be held at Triyuginarayan Temple. The rishis and devas were ecstatic to be attending the wedding of the universe's most eligible bachelor. It was a once-in-a-lifetime event and no one wanted to miss it.

The event's popularity was evident when a huge number of people turned up to see Shiva and Parvati tie the knot causing the earth to tilt to the north under their weight. The northern tilt caused a disturbance in the south. The rishis were worried about the adverse effects of the sudden shift. The matter came up before Shiva and he requested Sage Agastya to go down south to balance the weight between the north and south to reverse the tilt.

Sage Agastya, of course, left as instructed, but he was not happy about it. He, too, wanted to witness the divine wedding. Lord Shiva expressed his helplessness because Agastya was one of the best rishis and only he could handle the grave situation, which threatened to throw the planet off balance. He further reassured the sage that he would get married again in Kanchipuram just for Sage Agastya.

On this assurance, the sage left. The sand Shivalingam gradually hardened with time. Since Parvati sat under a mango tree, the Shivalingam came to be called Ekambareswarar, or the Lord of the Mango Tree. Another interesting feature of this thousand-year-old temple is the idols of Kubera, the god of wealth. He is on his vehicle, fish, and installed at twelve different spots in the temple to represent the twelve zodiac signs.

20

When Ganga met Narmada

Abrahman family once lived in a village. The husband, his wife, and their two sons. The brahman decided to visit Kashi, and while he was there, he left his body. The devastated family performed the last rites, and the brahman's wife took on the responsibility of bringing up the children. Years passed, and the brahman's wife, having fulfilled her responsibilities, awaited her death. Death, however, continued to escape her. Day by day, she became more and more forlorn. Her sons saw her misery and asked her what they could do to help.

The mother replied morosely, "I had desired to leave my body in Kashi, but that was not to be. Now I'm waiting for death here. After I'm gone, promise me that you will cast my bones in the holy waters of the Ganga. This alone will make me happy and it will also be good for you."

Mother's request seemed reasonable and doable, and the elder son gave her his word that he would carry out her last wish sincerely. Assured and relieved, she lived a few days chanting Lord Shiva's holy names and died thereafter. After performing the *shradha*, the son hired a servant, and they left with her bones to cast them in the Ganga.

They walked for twelve kilometres before they decided to rest for the night in a village called

Vimśatigrāma. They took shelter in a brahman's house. They had barely fallen asleep when the son heard a commotion in the courtyard.

The head of the house had returned home late. He noticed that the cow was tied in the courtyard without being milked. He called out to his wife to bring the calf so that the cow could be milked. The brahman tried to tie the calf to the peg near the cow but the calf was not hungry. She resisted being tied.

When the brahman continued urging the calf to drink the milk, the tired and irritated calf threw a tantrum and kicked the brahman. The brahman bent over, howling in pain. It was so unexpected that he couldn't believe what had hit him. He looked at the calf with growing rage unwilling to understand her obstinacy.

The pain had numbed his senses and compassion, fuelling his lower nature for control and combat. He picked up some wooden sticks lying nearby and attacked the calf. The helpless calf had no protection. She took all the hits. Neither the calf drank milk nor did the brahman milk the cow.

The cow stood motionless, watching the horrific scene. Her precious child was being assaulted in front of her. Big tears rolled down her cheeks as she groaned in pain. The exhausted calf looked at her and asked, "Mother, what makes you cry? What is troubling you? Pray tell me!"

The cow replied, "My child, this horrible man has beaten you. That is the cause of my distress. How can I bear it?"

The calf tried to relieve her mother's distress with the wisdom that she had heard from her, "We suffer as a result of our past actions. We spend our lives pursuing pleasure but the result of that is only misery. So, mother, no one but ourselves causes our misery."

The mother cow sighed. She knew the principles, yet, there was a searing pain in her heart. She had to do something about it. And there was only one way to abate that pain. She shared her thoughts, "My child, come morning, I will hit the brahman with my horns. No doubt he shall die unable to withstand the pain."

The calf was taken aback. Why was her mother doing this? "Mother, we are suffering now due to our earlier misdeeds. How much more will we suffer in the future by continuing with such acts?"

"I do not care about that," mother replied, "I know that my pain will only cease after I have taken revenge. After that, I know where I can go to dispel the sin of killing a brahman. So, do not despair."

The calf remained silent. There was nothing left to say.

The entire scene and conversation were being observed by the man who had taken shelter for the night in the same house. He was amazed to hear the cow's words. He definitely wanted to know where the cow would go to atone for her sins. He decided to wait and watch the events unfold the following day.

The next day he made an excuse that his servant had stomach pain and continued to stay in the house. He waited impatiently for what was to happen soon.

The brahman left home for some work and instructed his son to milk the cow. The son walked to the calf, untied her and then approached the infuriated cow who was waiting for her opportunity. As soon as he neared the cow, she hit the boy with her horns. So deadly was the lunge that the boy fell unconscious. Even before someone could give him water, he was dead.

The boy's mother too collapsed with grief. A large crowd gathered. By then the white cow had turned black. As people started pointing out this unusual phenomenon, the cow made her way out. The travelling man followed her.

The cow ran all the way to the River Narmada near Nandikesa shrine. She dipped three times in the river. Lo and behold! She was white once again and then she left. The man was now shocked. How holy was that place that could dispel the sin of brahman slaughter. He and his servant both took a bath there.

As they continued their journey, they couldn't stop talking about the marvellous river water. They had barely walked a few meters when they were accosted by a beautiful, young girl bedecked with ornaments.

She said, "You look like a brahman traveller. Where are you going and what is your purpose?"

The man was mesmerised by the girl's personality. He quickly told her about his mother's desire to cast her bones in the Ganga.

The divine girl said, "You have seen how the cow turned white by dispelling her sins here. You can cast her bones here too, in the holy spot. Why go elsewhere? As soon as you do it, you will see a beautiful form of your mother and she will attain her spiritual goals."

As the man reflected on her words, the girl further said, "In the month of Vaiśākha, on the auspicious seventh day in the bright half, Ganga comes here always. Today is that seventh day. The river is in the form of Ganga today."

Before the man could react to her words, the girl vanished into thin air. Right in front of him! She was none other than Ganga herself who had come to liberate his mother.

The man quickly did as he was told and true to the girl's words, his mother appeared in a divine form. She spoke to him, saying "I am pleased that you have kept your promise and done your duty. I bless you with prosperity and longevity. May your entire lineage flourish." The satisfied mother then departed for her heavenly abode with Lord Shiva's blessings.

There is an interesting reason behind why Ganga comes to meet Narmada in the month of Vaiśākha, on the auspicious seventh day in the bright half.

The story begins with a young brahman girl Rsika. She was extremely pious and a devotee of Lord Shiva. However, she became a widow very early in life. Her determination was such that even as widow, she lived a life of devotion to Lord Shiva, worshipping a Shivalingam made of mud.

Finding inner peace in worship and austerities, she kept herself busy but her world suddenly crashed with the arrival of a demon named Mudha. It was love at first sight for the lusty demon and he proposed to her. Rsika had noticed the demon's presence but she tried to ignore him.

Maybe her indifference would make him leave, she thought. Mudha tried to buy her love by offering many temptations but she continued to ignore his lewd comments and shameless overtures.

Her lack of response angered the demon and he erupted like a forest fire, wanting to consume her. Rsika was internally shivering, afraid that the demon would take advantage of her being alone. She chanted out her Lord's names beseeching him to protect her.

Shiva does not like to let down those who seek his protection. He appeared in front of her to annihilate the demon and give her joy. It only took a glance from him to turn Mudha into ashes. He then gazed affectionately at Rsika and gently cajoled her to ask for a boon.

Rsika did not want anything more than her safety. Which had already been ensured by Shiva. She only wanted to eternally remain his devotee. She folded her hands and thanked him profusely, singing his glories. He had saved not just her but many more by taking care of the demon. Shiva was impressed by her and granted her many boons.

Learning of Shiva's appearance in the forest, many demigods and celestials gathered around. Each one bowed and expressed their joy and prayers.

Ganga, the celestial river, too, was delighted with Rsika and expressed her feelings. "You must spend at least one day a year with me."

Rsika happily consented. Shiva merged into the Shivalingam and the holy place of Nandikesa became a vibrant centre of worship. Ganga voluntarily visits

Nandikesa and Narmada once a year to wipe off the sins that she collected from others.

By taking a bath in the Narmada on that day and worshiping Nandikesa, one can be freed from all sins like Brahma-hatya.

21

The Unfortunate King

The Ikshvaku Dynasty, or the Solar Dynasty, boasted of many great kings like Bharata, Harishchandra, Dilipa, Sagara, and Rama. The virtuous King Mitrasaha and his good wife Madayanti from the same dynasty are mentioned in the *Shiva Purana*. Like his ancestors, he too was an excellent archer and fond of hunting.

Hunting, though a benign sport pursued by many kings, became the cause of the many misfortunes in King Mitrasaha's life. During one hunting expedition with his huge army, the king came across Kamatha, an evil demon, in the forest. Everyone knew how Kamatha had created terror in the forest, harassing innocent men and sages. He was too cunning to be tracked, but that day, destiny presented him in front of King Mitrasaha. Taking aim, the king shot at the demon. A fierce battle erupted between the two stalwarts. King Mitrasaha emerged triumphant, killing the demon with his superior skills and strategies.

When the celebration had subsided, a humble young man approached the king. He wanted to serve the king by cooking for him. Liking his humility and gentle manner, the king hired him instantly, bypassing the rules and regulations of working in the palace.

This was a huge mistake because, unknown to the king, the lad was not an ordinary human but the slayed demon's younger brother. He was exploding with anger at the death of his brother at the hands of the king. Seeking revenge, he cooked up this plot well aware that a face-to-face combat with the king would result in a similar disaster for himself. The king had not hired a decent employee but a wolf in sheep's skin.

Days passed. One day, the king instructed the new cook to prepare for Shradha. Shradha is a religious duty that involves repaying debts to one's ancestors. The king wanted to ensure that all his guests were fed a sumptuous meal that day. His guru, Sage Vashistha was a special invitee. The demon in disguise was waiting for an opportunity like this to turn the tables on the king. Amongst the large number of dishes that he had prepared, he also added human flesh to them. Moreover, he served human flesh to the most important guest, Sage Vashistha.

The minute the plate was served, the eminent guru sensed the outrageous prank. He assumed it was the doing of his host, King Mitrasaha. Without giving him a chance to explain his innocence, the sage erupted like a volcano. He said, "Since you have served human flesh to me, I curse you to turn into a flesh-eating demon."

His fiery curse was the hot lava flowing on the king's body. Fumbling for words and shocked at the injustice meted out to him, the king explained that it was his cook who had done the mischief, not him. By then, the sage had calmed down enough to understand what had transpired. A curse, however, cannot be reversed. The sage, on the other hand, changed the curse to last twelve years.

This was not enough to erase the pain in King Mitrasaha's heart. It was impossible to accept the sudden turn of events and the life that now awaited him as a demon. He groped around to get hold of water in his palm and was ready to counter-curse the sage for the haste he had shown in punishing him unnecessarily.

His wife, Madyanti, was quick to hold his hand and prevent him from committing another sin, this time intentionally. She fell at his feet imploring him to resist from doing something as catastrophic as cursing his preceptor. Fortunately, the king came to his senses and dropped the water on his feet causing his feet to become deformed.

Soon, the curse took its effect transforming the elegant royal king into a cannibalistic *rakshasa*. Resembling Yama, the demon wandered around in forests, devouring men, and other creatures. He came across a newly married Brahman couple who were engrossed in each other's love. He pounced on the man, eager to eat him. The woman shrieked at the sudden intrusion into their private moment and begged the monster to spare her husband. They had barely begun their life together. The monster simply laughed at the woman's pathetic appeals. Words penetrated his thick skull as much as water penetrates oil.

Just like a tiger seizes a deer, the demon grabbed the young brahman boy and that was the end of his life. The woman sobbed her heart out unable to deal with the tragedy. She slowly got up to arrange for a funeral for the remains of his body and resolved to enter the pyre herself. Before giving up her body, she cursed the demonic king.

"If you unite with a woman, or embrace her, you too will see your end."

The twelve years ended, and the demon regained his kingly form and returned to the palace. Although there was celebration all around and the king himself was happy, he could not share his love with his wife, Madyanti. Queen Madyanti knew about the curse and did not allow the king to come near her, fearing the worst. It was better to remain at a distance than become a widow.

With the passage of time, the king became restless. He had lost interest in his duties and in life itself, owing to his brahma-hatya sin. All kingly pleasures paled before thoughts of the price he would have to pay for the atrocious sin he had committed. To atone for all his sins, he tried chanting, sacrifices, holy rites, and rituals; but nothing gave him peace of mind.

In search of something deeper, he left his kingdom and reached Mithila. Once there, providence led him to the most exalted of sages, Gautama Rishi. Just the vision of Gautama Rishi erased the fountainhead of pain that had been constantly bubbling inside him. His serene countenance, his kind gestures—everything about him conveyed inner peace.

For the first time in many decades, the king felt a wave of tranquillity sweeping over him. He bowed to the sage again and again. When the sage asked about his well-being, the damn of constraint broke, letting out the agony he had kept inside all these years, since sage Vashistha cursed him.

He concluded by telling the sage about the last straw that broke him completely. "The sin of brahma-hatya is a big load upon me. Even after performing thousands of purificatory rites, I am unable to wash it off my conscience. Is it because I am an out and out a sinful soul?"

As the sage looked at him compassionately, the king poured out his heart, "In the last few minutes after having met you, I feel that I have attained the purpose of my life. Your presence is as soothing as a balm to a painful injury. Please give me shelter at your lotus feet so I can be at peace for the rest of my life."

Gautama Rishi, understanding the king's plight, revealed his wisdom to him. "O' King, sin no longer and seek refuge in Lord Shiva," he said. Lord Shiva never forsakes his devotees. Do what I say. Now listen carefully.

"Go to Gokarna on the shore of the western oceans and pray at the Mahabala temple. Shiva is present there as Mahabala. He is greater than your greatest sins. Whatever your sin may be, he is the destroyer of them. Take a dip in the holy waters there and meditate on the Lord. Whoever does so is sure to attain the abode of Shiva.

"O' King, now do as I say. Worship Shiva in Gokarna and get rid of your sinful burdens."

The king was delighted with the sage's solution. He could now see light at the end of the dark tunnel. Taking the sage's blessings, he literally ran to Gokarna. True to the sage's words, after ceremonial ablutions in the holy pond and worship of Lord Shiva, King Mitrasaha left for the divine abode. That is the wonderful power of Mahabala, which dispels all sins.

22

Mahakaleshwar

Ujjain, in Madhya Pradesh, is a historical city that holds great significance in ancient religious scriptures. References to Avanti, as it was known then, are found in the *Ramayana, Mahabharata,* Shiva Purana, and *Skanda Purana.* It is believed that Lord Rama, in the Treta yuga, visited Avanti along with Sita Devi to perform the rites (*Pinda daana*) of his father, King Dasharatha. In Dwapara yuga, Krishna and Sudama studied in the ashrama of Sandipani muni in Ujjain.

There lived a brahman in Avanti called Vedapriya. For twenty-four hours a day, he was absorbed in the study of the Vedas and performing Vedic rites in devotion to Lord Shiva. He was a happy man because he had four sons and all four had taken after him. Devapriya was the eldest son, followed by Priyamedha, Suvrita, and Suvrata. They were as knowledgeable as their father and spent a good amount of their time worshiping Shiva. Avanti flourished under the auspices of such learned brahmans who continually performed yagyas for the welfare of the city.

In the nearby hills of Ratnamala, lived a powerful asura, Dusana. He had obtained many boons from Lord Brahma. Thanks to these boons, his evil nature multiplied exponentially, disturbing the balance between good and evil. He wreaked havoc throughout the universe, seizing control of all planets and forcing godly people to flee and hide.

Having returned from world conquests, he noticed that there was religion prevailing in his own backyard, Avanti. Intolerant of even a speck of Vedic sacrifices, he launched a full-scale attack on the city. Brahmans were his enemies and primary targets, and it gave him sweet satisfaction to interrupt the sacrifices happening in Avanti. One by one, every house where yagyas were being performed was destroyed. He issued blanket orders to stop all religious activities or perish. His goal was to eliminate dharma from the face of the earth.

He called upon four of his best men and instructed them to comb the city of Avanti and enforce his rules. Anyone found offering worship to God was to be destroyed immediately. The news spread like wildfire, and all Vedic rituals came to a standstill. No one dared go against the wishes of Dusana, lest they lose their lives. No one, but the four brahman sons. Devapriya, Priyamedha, Suvrita, and Suvrata.

None of them had an iota of fear. They simply went on with their routine practices of yagya and meditation on Lord Shiva, oblivious to the chaos around them. When Shiva was with them, who could harm them? While the whole city was in turmoil, the four brahmans bravely marched on with full faith that Shiva would protect them.

Vedapriya said to his sons, "Our city is being ransacked and tortured by the asuras but we do not have an army to protect us. We have no weapons to fight back and defeat the wicked elements and drive them away. We have only

Lord Shiva with us. Lord Shiva is the only shelter for his devotees. Let us not waver in our faith, but rather continue to worship the Lord."

Encouraged by their father's words, the brahmans performed worship of their Shivalingam made of earth. Theirs was the only house in Avanti that had challenged Dusana's orders. They were so engrossed that they were praying to Lord Shiva even as Dusana stood at their door baying for their blood.

"Capture them! Kill them!", yelled asura Dusana at his army. The army broke into their house with swords in their hands, thirsting for blood. Vedapriya and his sons remained stationary because they, in fact, had not heard anything at all. They were unaware of their physical surroundings, lost in another dimension of existence. As Dusana inched closer to them to strike the erring men, he was pushed back by a sudden creaking sound.

It felt as if something was being torn open. Simultaneously, the ground beneath them began to rumble and shake, throwing them off balance. They all fell on each other. What followed gave the hardened, battle-seasoned, and trained to be stoic in the face of suffering, asuras, goosebumps. The scene unfolding was a first in their life.

Rising from underground through the crack in the earth, was the huge hideous form of Lord Shiva. He was Mahakala, the saviour of his devotees and the slayer of his adversaries. He had emerged from a chasm, "You have dared to harass my devotees thinking they are helpless. You were wrong. Now run as fast as you can to save yourself."

The asuras did not need another warning to do as they were told. The gruesome Mahakala was so terrifying that they ran helter-skelter. Mahakala allowed them to run a distance and then with his fierce gaze, burnt them to ashes. The once-mighty Dusana had shrunk to the size of a handful of ash.

Like the sun dispelling night-long darkness, Mahakala had destroyed the asuras. Demigods gathered dotting the skyline, celebrating the triumph of good over evil. The sounds of bugles and drums reverberated in the air and flower petals showered down on Lord Shiva. Conches were blown to herald all auspiciousness. The brahman brothers rejoiced to see their worship fructifying in front of them. Paying obeisance with folded hands, they sang glories of their deity.

Lord Shiva wanted to bless them with a boon of their choice. Unanimously, they asked for liberation from the ocean of material existence. Also wanting to help others, they asked Mahakala to stay there and become accessible for worship. His presence would help many others find their goal in life.

Shiva acceded to their wishes. The brahmans attained liberation and Shiva remained in the chasm from which he had emerged, to protect his devotees. The Shivalingam with a base of three kilometres in all directions, is worshipped as Mahakaleshwara. Darshan of Mahakaleshwara grants fulfilment of all desires in life and salvation thereafter. On seeing the image, no one will be miserable even in dreams.

Another legend from the *Shiva Purana* revolving around Mahakaleshwara, talks about King Chandrasena, who ruled the city of Avanti. Extremely learned in Vedic scriptures, he was a sincere devotee of Lord Shiva. Manibhadra, the chief gana of Lord Shiva, was his friend. Happy with his devotion, Manibhadra gifted King Chandrasena the precious *Chintamani* jewel.

The Chintamani was no less than *Kaustubha*, the divine jewel that adorned Lord Vishnu. The effulgence from Chintamani was blinding as it shone like the brilliant sun. Any metal that came into contact with it, whether tin or copper or any other, miraculously turned into gold! So powerful was its association!

When King Chandrasena wore it around his neck, it seemed that he himself was divinely refulgent, radiating a brilliant golden aura. The natural simplicity of his devotion to Lord Shiva coupled with the divinity of Chintamani, made him appear extraordinary, almost like a god.

But in this world, personal success breeds a certain amount of greed and jealousy in others. Envy reared its ugly head in the neighbouring kingdoms when they heard about the miraculous Chintamani stone in King Chandrasena's possession.

Why should he be the one with the magical stone and not them? Many kings spent sleepless nights wanting the jewel for themselves and plotting various schemes to obtain it. And some kings had the audacity to go to King Chandrasena and ask him to hand over the jewel to them.

Amused and miffed, King Chandrasena naturally refused to part with it. This created more agitation in the hearts of the rebuffed kings, strengthening their resolve to acquire the precious gem by hook or by crook. They all got together to form an alliance to attack Avanti and conquer the kingdom. United, they could achieve what they had failed to do individually.

The massive army surrounded Avanti from all sides. Their numbers were so huge that King Chandrasena knew his army would not be able to sustain the battle for too long. Any attempt to counter the siege would be futile. Being a devotee of Shiva, he went to Mahakaleshwara to pray to him. If Shiva wanted, there could be a way to save Avanti.

The king immersed himself deeply in worshipping his deity. Night and day, he sat in the temple without food and water, seeking Lord Shiva's guidance and intervention. Not for a moment did his faith in Shiva flicker. Faith, he knew, could move mountains. Unknown to him, Shiva was pleased with him and was indeed up to something. He never let his devotees' faith go in vain.

While the king was performing his puja, he was being watched. By a five-year-old boy who had come with his mother to herd their cows. The boy was fascinated with the scene in front of him. Every movement of the king was like poetry in action and he was as immersed in the worship as the king was. His mother, a cowherdess and recently widowed, was also watching in rapture.

Finally, they snapped out of their reverie and returned home. Home was a camp, a shelter for homeless people. The king worshipping Mahakala was stuck in the boy's mind and he thought to enact the scene by himself. He hunted for a suitable pebble to be used as a Shivalingam. He also found suitable objects to represent lamp, incense, rice, cloth, ornaments, and the other paraphernalia that he had seen being used for *arti*. Using leaves and flowers, he took much delight in worshipping his make-shift Shivalingam. He danced and offered obeisance to his innocent heart's content. He did it again and again to experience the soothing effect it had on him.

His absorption in Lord Shiva made him oblivious to his mother's calls. She had been calling him continually to have his meal but the boy had not even heard her. This infuriated the mother and she marched up to him angrily. She was angered further seeing he was engaged in frivolous dancing and chanting. Thinking it to be lack of discipline, she thrashed him without remorse. The poor boy fell to the ground writhing in pain. He called out to Lord Shiva for help and after sobbing with pain, fell asleep there itself.

The next day, when he woke up, he did not know where he was. His surroundings had changed and instead of the shelter, he was in a huge mansion. Eyes wide open, he looked around. There was opulence everywhere. The mud floor had turned into an exclusive marble floor. The thatched walls were embedded with gems. Gold coins and precious gems were scattered across the floor. Every corner had a golden jug carrying juice while soft music played in the background.

In the centre was a jewel bedecked Shivalingam, the one he had played with so joyfully. He saw Shiva emerge from there; he blessed him and vanished again. The boy realised the lingam was the centre of all mercy.

When his mother returned with the cows, she too was shocked to see the new abode waiting for her. Mother and son hugged and pinched each other to check if it was real or a dream. If it was a dream, they never wanted to wake up. They finally concluded it was a blessing from Lord Shiva who was pleased with his little devotee's worship.

Word spread like fire about the miraculous happening in Avanti. A crowd gathered around to see the power of faith. News reached King Chandrasena who hurried to the lavish mansion to meet the divine boy. Singing the glories of Lord Shiva, the king hugged the boy, happy to have the darshan of someone blessed by Mahakala himself.

Spies carried the unbelievable news to the liaising kings who were waiting to strike the kingdom. But the news made them pause and think. Here was a king and a kingdom that seemed to be fully blessed by divine powers. While the king had been gifted the transcendental jewel, even ordinary citizens evoked magical gifts routinely from celestial powers.

How prudent was it to attack such an invincible kingdom protected by higher powers, and risk defeat? If God himself was on their side, who could defeat King Chandrasena? In fact, they thought, they might attract Shiva's wrath by their actions. In unanimous agreement, they abandoned their enmity and entered the kingdom with flags of truce and went to Mahakala to worship him.

The next they met the miraculous boy in the heavenly home. There King Chandrasena welcomed them. The kings offered rich gifts to the boy and worshipped the Shivalingam.

Later, the boy was declared the chief of all the cowherd communities. Hanuman then appeared in the king's court and said, "This boy has the blessings of Lord Shiva and will bring glory to his lineage. In the eighth generation, there will be a cowherd called Nanda and his son will be Krishna, an incarnation of Vishnu." Making this prophecy, Hanuman then disappeared leaving behind the dazed and ecstatic citizens of Avanti.

23

Ghushmesha

In a splendorous mountain terrain named Deva, in the southern part of the country, lived a brahman named Sudharma who belonged to the Bharadwaja descendance. Sudeha was his beloved wife and they were an ideal couple, engaged in constantly serving the society and the Gods. They especially worshipped Lord Shiva with great zeal and faith.

With a lot of prosperity, opportunity, and abundance, Sudharma and his wife lived happily. Of course, though it seemed as though they had everything, they were sad about one thing and that was the absence of a son that would carry forward their legacy. Though Sudharma took in the lack of a child through a more philosophical approach, Sudeha was emotionally affected and could not understand the philosophy of destiny that Sudharma would every now and then come up with.

Not a day passed without Sudeha nagging Sudharma to do something about their problem. This made Sudharma feel more and more inclined towards his spiritual practices. He kept giving her advice to steer her intelligence towards higher thoughts rather than worry.

One day things became really complicated when Sudeha picked up an ugly quarrel with the neighbour. The matter was really trivial but the neighbour complicated it by saying things she should never have.

She pierced Sudeha where it hurt the most. She said, "O barren woman, what makes you so arrogant? Do you have a son like me to inherit your wealth and prosperity? When you die, your property will the confiscated by the king and your wealth will be emptied into the royal coffers."

These words tormented Sudeha just like a scorpion bite torments a person long after the event. It drove her into depression. She couldn't handle the pain of not having a child anymore. She shared her terrible experience with her husband and expected him to understand her predicament.

Instead, Sudharma took a more practical approach. He began to preach to her about the power of destiny and the helplessness of a human in the presence of it. When she saw that her husband wasn't taking her seriously, she threatened to end her life if he didn't help her conceive a child.

In order to make her see reason, Sudharma chose two flowers and offered them to Lord Shiva. Offering intense prayers for direction, he asked Sudeha to choose one of the flowers. He had chosen the right-side flower as the one that would mean that they would have a son. Sudeha offered a prayer and made her choice. But when she made her selection, she selected the left-side flower, which clearly indicated that it was Shiva's direction that they would not have a son.

Sudeha knew that these predictions would never be wrong and that her husband was an expert in these rituals. But yet she persisted in her arguments. This time she took a different approach. She proposed that since they were destined not to have a child, why not consider marrying another woman and beget a child through her?

Sudharma was shocked at her proposal. Why was she being so obstinate? He decided to focus on his worship to Lord Shiva and ignore her constant nagging.

One day she did something unbelievable. She brought her sister and insisted that her husband marry her to beget a child through her. Sudharma was stunned at his wife's appalling suggestion. He pointed out to her that she was making this proposal out of her obsession for a child, but if he did marry and her sister gave birth to a son, then she would surely get jealous. Sudeha joined her palms and humbly begged her husband to accede to this request. She promised him that she would never be jealous of her own sister.

Seeing the insistence of Sudeha and the eager acceptance of the proposal by her sister Ghushma, Sudharma agreed. The marriage ceremony took place immediately and the three of them lived together in harmony focusing on their worship of Lord Shiva as their primary purpose and everything else as secondary.

Ghushma followed some strict austerities to beget a child. Every single day she made 101 earthen dolls and worshipped them according to sacred rituals and eventually threw them in a lake nearby. Sudeha helped her with all these efforts as she had found great hope in having an offspring through her sister.

Along with the ritual of worshipping and offering 101 dolls into the lake every day, Ghushma also worshipped an image of Lord Shiva that she would create every day. She continued her worship relentlessly till she completed the worship of 100,000 images of Lord Shiva over a period of time. The result of that worship was believed to surely gift a child.

By the grace of Lord Shiva and as a result of the great sincerity with which she carried out all the rituals, Ghushma was blessed with a son. The child was extremely beautiful and was endowed with a plethora of divine qualities. Sudharma was delighted to hold his son in his arms. What especially pleased him was that the birth chart of the child predicted that he would go on to be a great soul with divine virtues.

Initially Sudeha was equally thrilled with the arrival of the little baby. But as people in the village began to celebrate the son and his mother, her prominence took a backseat. In fact, no one really bothered about her. Every discussion was centred only around her sister Ghushma and her son. Sudeha's heart began to blaze with extreme jealousy.

As days passed, the hatred in Sudeha's heart grew in epic proportions. She was just not able to handle her sister's happiness. While the village continued to celebrate the birth of that child, she just couldn't bear to even look at the little baby. As the child grew, her hatred grew. She began to isolate herself from the family and spent more and more time alone seething in anger.

Eventually the boy grew into a handsome young man and became the talk of the town. Many marriage proposals came his way and he was considered the most eligible bachelor in that village. In the meanwhile, Sudharma had gotten very close to Ghushma. It was not that he neglected Sudeha but somehow her mindset had become highly negative and critical. She felt that her husband was neglecting her and she was convinced that the boy was the root cause of all her misery.

In due course the boy was married to an extremely beautiful girl. The arrival of the daughter-in-law at the house heralded even more misery for Sudeha. Though the daughter-in-law and son offered equal respect to both the mothers, somehow Sudeha felt that she was the neglected person in the family.

One day she made a decision that was too harsh. She felt that her entire life had gone waste and was turning into a long spell of misery. The only way she could get relief from all this misery was if she saw tears in the eyes of her ever-smiling sister Ghushma.

That night, Sudeha entered the room where the boy was sleeping with a dagger in her hands. Without a second thought, Sudeha drove the knife into the heart of the sleeping boy and killed him. Then she slashed off every limb of his body in great anger. Packing the boy's chopped limbs in a bag, she carried them and threw them into the lake where her sister had deposited the clay dolls during her worship.

When she threw the mortal remains of the boy into that lake, she felt a sense of relief. A relief that she had reversed destiny. The boy had gone back to the very place from which he came from. She returned home and slept peacefully.

The next morning when the family realised the horror of what had happened overnight, they were bewildered and aghast. They could see blood and gore all over the room, but they couldn't figure how it all happened. There was no trace of the boy or his body. Thus, they couldn't even conclude that he was dead. A pitiable cry rose from the daughter-in-law's throat, soothing Sudeha's stony heart. She smiled internally while pretending to cry. Of course, she was waiting to see Ghushma cry.

But that never happened. Somehow, she was made of a different mettle. She kept saying that the one who gave her the son would protect her son. She had great faith in Lord Shiva and even in sorrow she continued her worship. After completing the ritual, she took the image of Lord Shiva to the lake. Going deep into the lake, chanting the holy names of Shiva, she reverentially deposited the image into the water and returned. When she stepped out onto the shore, a surprise was awaiting her.

Ghushma saw her son standing on the banks of the lake completely unharmed and lustrously effulgent in form. The son explained to her that he had died. But the power of her prayers and the grace of Lord Shiva had gifted him a second chance. Ghushma wasn't really surprised because she had complete faith in the grace of Lord Shiva. Why would she be surprised when she wasn't even shocked at his demise? She had reached a stage of equilibrium and wasn't affected by joy or sorrow anymore.

Just then the brilliant form of Lord Shiva materialised before them out of thin air. He began to speak to the grateful mother and son. He told Ghushma that he was extremely delighted with her devotion and dedication. He wanted to offer her a boon. He additionally suggested that since that wicked lady had done the heinous act of killing an innocent boy, he would eliminate her with his trident.

Reverentially offering her respects to Lord Shiva, Ghushma spoke the following words. "O my Lord, I request you to protect my sister Sudeha. Please do not harm her in any way."

Shiva was shocked at this request. Why would she want to protect someone who caused her so much pain and perpetrated such a heinous act of violence? Such an aggressor must be punished, Lord Shiva opined. Ghushma smiled and explained her thoughts.

She said, "My dear Lord, the moment you descend anywhere, how can sin exist there? Moreover, sin cannot exist in a place where forgiveness exists. When a person who is harmed decides to help the person who harms him, that very moment sin ceases to exist."

Never before had he heard such compassionate words. Lord Shiva was highly impressed by the answer and realised that this lady was highly elevated in her thinking. Pleased with her, Shiva told her that since she was free of human vices, he would like to offer her another boon of her choice. Immediately, Ghushma made a uniquely different request. She said, "If you desire to give me a boon, I request you to stay at this very place. Let it be so that you are recognised by my name and you remain here protecting the world."

Lord Shiva was thrilled at this unique request of his devotee Ghushma. With a smile on his face, he said, "As you desire, I shall stay here and be known by your name. The world will know me as *Ghushmesha* and I will confer happiness on everyone who worships me sincerely. My lingam form here will be world famous. This lake will be known to the world as *Shivalaya* and will grant all the desires of anyone who merely glances at it.

"I also bless you that for up to 101 generations in your family, sons of great excellence will be born and they will live with great satisfaction, prosperity, and excellence. They will not only be learned but also be kind. They will have great happiness while they live and attain liberation on death."

As soon as he said this, Lord Shiva disappeared and in his place was a Shivalingam that came to be known as Ghushmesha. The lake was henceforth called Shivalaya. Sudharma and his two wives along with their son and daughter-in-law went around the lingam 101 times and worshipped it with all their hearts. All the negativity and hatred in their minds disappeared.

Sudeha was ashamed that she had behaved so insanely. Once the cloud in her mind had disappeared, she returned to her normal self. She begged forgiveness from her family for her cruelty and selfishness.

This deity of Ghushmesha is considered one of the twelve Jyotirlingams across the globe and is believed to be a powerful yielder of all desires in this world and liberation after death. Every time one remembers the story of the appearance of this Jyotirlingam, one should meditate on the devotion of Ghushma and her forgiving nature. Only love has the power to conquer hatred.

24

Nandishwar Mahadeva

The moment he stepped into Vrindavan, a fragrant cool breeze caressed his face. He had to close his eyes and take in the feel of divinity in his very first step into the holy land. His locks of matted hair gently waved as if dancing in joy. A joy that seeped through every inch of Shiva's robust body. The ashes smeared across his body gave him the look of detachment. He hardly cared for material looks because he was so absorbed in the highest spiritual truths. Where there was any element of spiritual truth, Shiva surely ventured there to experience it.

That was his primary reason to step into the holy land of Vrindavan today. There was a tiny little truth that was waiting to be discovered. Shiva couldn't help but smile thinking of the joy he would feel in the presence of this most powerful secret of the universe.

He walked briskly towards his destination. He didn't need to ask anyone for direction as he himself was the master of all directions. There was nothing in this world that Shiva did not know. Yet, there was something in that little village of Vrindavan named Nandagaon that was intriguing to Shiva. So intriguing that he ran out of his divine abode Kailash in the north and hurried through a tiny hamlet in a disguise that he had never ever tried in the past.

Yes, Shiva was disguised today. There was nothing he had ever needed to hide from. There was nothing that he had ever not understood. But here was an itsy-bitsy secret that he was so eager to decipher that he was ready to hide his real identity as Shiva and take on the guise of a mendicant begging for alms. Of course, what he came to beg for was something else!

As he edged closer to the palace of King Nanda in Nandagaon, his palpitation increased considerably and so did his excitement. Villagers stepped out of his path and reverentially bowed down as he walked with rapid strides, climbing up the windy path that led to the palace gates. Finally, he was there! In his excitement to get in, he wasn't able to speak coherently. Tears welled up his eyes as his voice too deserted him by choking up.

The palace guards were unable to comprehend what the strange looking personality was trying to communicate. A commotion followed and in sheer frustration, Shiva began to play on his damru (a tiny little hand drum that is shaken to create sound) creating a very significant noise that reached right into the palace courtyard.

Mother Yashoda heard the strange sound of the damru and stepped out into the porch. When she saw the guards stopping the yogi, she walked up to him and asked him what he wanted. In response, Shiva smiled. He openly told her that he was here only to see her little son. The words caused tremendous anxiety in Yashoda. Her over-protective motherly instincts stepped in.

She inspected the stranger. From top to bottom he was covered with ashes, his hair appeared matted and coarse. His neck was encircled by deadly poisonous snakes. Scorpions fearlessly roamed all over his body creating a creepy sight. Every few seconds, a spider would peep out of his hair locks. Yashoda couldn't imagine the impact of the vision of this scary-looking stranger on her little one. She didn't want the stranger to go anywhere near her little blue boy. Refusing vehemently, she ran in and slammed the door shut.

But Shiva was in no mood to give up so easily. In a loud voice, he kept beseeching her to let him have one glance at her baby boy. He kept begging that he had come a long distance for just a little glimpse of that divine boy. Mother Yashoda closed her ears with her hands and kept refusing the request. There was no way she would allow that strange yogi to scare her little darling. Sensing her adamancy, Shiva declared that he would sit outside the palace all day, till the little boy Krishna himself came out.

A few hours passed in silence. Mother Yashoda felt a wee bit guilty about having treated a guest so badly. But her heart refused to compromise on her son's safety. She peeped out of the palace window and saw the yogi seated on the ground right outside the palace gates. His eyes were closed and his back was erect. With his legs folded in lotus posture, the yogi was immersed in deep meditation. There was a slight smile on his otherwise serious face.

Yashoda stepped out of the palace gates and walking up to the yogi, dropped some food into his bowl. Hearing the food plop into his bowl, the yogi opened his eyes. Seeing mother Yashoda in front of him gave some hope to his mind. He smiled weakly. His eyes begged her for the fulfilment of his desire. But she was still extremely firm.

Refusing to change her stand, she said, "I know you yogis are always hungry. I have given you some food. Please go away from here now."

Shiva plunged into despair. All hope had left, and he quietly stood up and walked away from Nanda Bhavan. Reaching a nearby forest, he found shelter under a tree. With tears flowing down his face, Shiva began to meditate on that form of the Supreme Lord that he was craving to see. He was abjectly unhappy at being denied that supreme fortune.

Hoping against hope, he prayed intensely for divine grace to descend on him. The place where Lord Shiva sat praying intensely with great hope for one little glimpse of baby Krishna came to be known as the forest of hope or Asheshwar Van and this form of Shiva meditating for a spark of hope to descend into his life came to be known as Asheshwar Mahadeva.

In the meanwhile, Nanda Bhavan was going through a mini-crisis. Krishna was crying intensely. The little baby wasn't just crying, he was wailing. Mother Yashoda had never seen her little child wail so hard. She tried every possible trick in the book to get her baby to stop. But nothing seemed to work.

In fact, the more she tried, the harder he cried. She invited all the elderly gopis who were more experienced than her in handling babies. The more they tried, the more he cried. None of them could calm the wailing baby.

Dark clouds of concern engulfed Nanda Bhavan. While the drama intensified throwing everyone into a cauldron of anxiety, an elderly gopi was stirring some thoughts. Satisfied, she approached Yashoda and held her hand. With a look of concern, she said, "Someone has surely cast an evil eye on our little one. Tell me the names of those who have visited the palace and seen little Krishna. Don't leave out any name."

Thinking carefully, Yashoda recalled the names of Abhinanda, Sunanda and Vrishabhanu Maharaj. But these people were family and they loved Krishna so much. Why would they cast an evil eye on him? Wait! Suddenly she remembered the strange-looking yogi who was loitering around the palace with great eagerness to see the baby.

Animatedly she explained to the elderly gopi about her experience with the fearsome-looking yogi who was covered all over in ashes and had various kinds of creepy creatures crawling around his body.

On hearing the description, immediately the elderly gopi zoomed on the cause of distress and confirmed that he was definitely the one who cast a spell on the child due to the harsh denial of his wish. She demanded to know where the yogi was at present. But Yashoda had no idea. Immediately, small batches of gopis were dispatched all around Nandagaon to find the mystic sage.

When they finally found him seated under a tree in the forest nearby, they walked up to him and requested him to come to Nanda Bhavan as mother Yashoda was calling for him. Shiva smiled. Grace finally! With great joy he sprinted to the same palace where he had initially been refused entry.

Mother Yashoda was furious with him and she demanded that the yogi do the needful to remove the evil eye and calm her hysterically crying baby. Shiva nodded his head and came forward. That's when he got the first glimpse of little Krishna innocently sprawled on a cradle holding his tiny feet and crying. Tears began to pour down Shiva's cheeks. He had never seen such beauty in his life. Krishna was a compact bundle of divine joy.

Mother Yashoda begged him to cure her child and get him to stop crying. Shiva knew that he had full control over the situation and could get away with anything. He looked at the crying baby seriously and said that there was only one way to cure the problem. The gopis were curious and eager to hear the solution. Shiva said, "The crying will stop as soon as the little baby puts his little feet on my head."

Mother Yashoda was aghast. There was no way she would allow that. There were snakes around his neck plus so many scorpions on the matted hair of the uncouth mendicant. She could not possibly expose her child to such dangers. But the elderly gopi held her hand and restrained her from speaking.

Gauging the situation was in his favour, Lord Shiva stepped forward, bent over the cradle and placed his head lower, inches away from the feet of the divine baby. Gently touching the feet of Krishna, he closed his eyes to place the little feet on his head. As soon as Krishna's feet was placed on his head, Lord Shiva felt a jolt of ecstasy and his entire body trembled. Standing up again, he began to dance in great bliss while playing his damru. Seeing the wild dance of Lord Shiva, little Krishna began to laugh. He seemed so blissful enjoying the dance of this divine yogi.

Taken aback by the effect the dance of Lord Shiva had on her little child, mother Yashoda requested him to stay in

Nanda Bhavan forever. Whenever Krishna cried, she wanted Shiva to come and take care of the little child. Shiva agreed, obviously happily; but he placed two conditions.

His first condition was that whenever Krishna was bathed, a little water from that bathing should be sprinkled on him. And his second condition was that whenever Krishna ate food, the remnants of that food must be offered to him immediately. Only when Yashoda agreed to both these conditions did Shiva agree to stay. He promised her that in his presence, no demoniac forces would ever come to Nandagaon and disturb little Krishna.

That form of Lord Shiva that is stationed in Nandagaon is known as Nandishwar Mahadeva and even to this day, both his conditions are diligently taken care of and he protects the village of Nandagaon.

25

Bhubaneshwar

Some people are difficult to please and some people are very difficult to please. Some people are easy to please and yet some others are very easy to please. Lord Shiva is called Ashutosh because he falls in the category of personalities who are very easy to please. He has such a soft heart that he gets very pleased even with a little exhibition of sincerity. Of course, not everyone approaches him with a sincere heart. But Lord Shiva chooses not to see anyone's wrong intentions but rather gives the benefit of doubt to those who approach him.

The king of Kashi was one such that performed great austerities to win the favour of Lord Shiva. Pleased with him, Shiva offered him any boon he desired. His only desire was to conquer Lord Krishna in a battle. Shiva winced at hearing that request. Yet another demon bearing grudges and harbouring revenge fantasies against the Supreme Lord. Where do these demons keep coming from? Lord Shiva wondered. But anyway, he had a promise to keep. He instructed the king to go ahead and attack Krishna and he would follow behind closely to offer support.

Fortunately for the king, Krishna happened to be in Kashi at that very moment, totally unaware of this conspiracy. The king of Kashi gathered his army and left to fight against Krishna. As promised Lord Shiva followed closely along with his followers.

When Krishna saw two huge armies marching towards him threateningly, he simply raised his arm and invoked the all-powerful Sudarshan chakra. The moment that chakra was released, it beheaded the King of Kashi. It didn't stop there. It went on to slaughter the whole army of the king and even went on to massacre the army of Lord Shiva. Within moments, the length and breadth of Kashi's battleground had turned into a crematorium.

Seeing everyone dead in an instant, Lord Shiva became furious. He threw his most powerful weapon, the Pasupatastra towards the raging disc that was still thirsty for blood. Instead of neutralising the disc, the Pasupatastra became dysfunctional.

When he saw his supreme weapon ineffective in front of the disc of Krishna, Shiva realised that there was little else he could do. Of course, Shiva loved Krishna. Between them there was great appreciation and respect, but due to the promise he had rendered to the king of Kashi, Shiva had ended up confronting Krishna.

Now that the king of Kashi was no more, his commitment was also no more. He rushed towards Krishna and began to offer beautiful prayers filled with love and devotion. He pleaded Krishna's forgiveness for attacking him, rather than welcoming him as a guest in Kashi. But now it was too late and Kashi was no longer fit for the residence of Lord Shiva. He begged Krishna to forgive his mistake and suggest an alternate place for him to reside in.

Krishna instantly smiled. There was no way he could retain any sort of anger or animosity towards Lord Shiva.

"Towards the north of my most holy abode Purushottam Kshetra or Jagannath Puri, is the most holy land known as Ekamra Kanan. The land is so potent that anyone stepping into it can simultaneously attain *bhakti* and *mukti*. I hereby offer you that holy land of Ekamra Kanan. Please reside there and from there guard Purushottam Kshetra. The world will know you as Bhubaneshwar, which means the Lord of the world. You will also be known as Bhakti Pradata. Anyone worshipping you there will attain devotion towards me. Anyone who worships you in Ekamra Kanan, will have access to my abode Purushottam Kshetra."

Though the experience was embarrassing, Lord Shiva chose to see the positive side of it and focused on the blessing of being able to reside so close to Sri Purushottam Kshetra. He rushed back to share this news with Parvati, his eternal companion.

When Parvati absorbed the glories of Ekamra Kanan, she became fascinated. She wanted to immediately visit that holy place. Lord Shiva instructed her to proceed ahead and told her that he would be joining her soon after completing some responsibilities at Kashi. Riding her favourite vehicle, the lion, Parvati arrived at Ekamra Kanan and was fascinated by its beauty and majestic landscape. To her it seemed to be more pleasing than even Kailash, their original home.

While she was strolling around casually enjoying the natural beauty of that place, she experienced something that thrilled her. Right in the middle of the beautiful city, was the most magnificent Lingam that she had ever seen in her life.

She was so happy to see the Lingam had manifested there much before the arrival of her husband. This Lingam was lustrous and was emanating a white and black effulgence. Instantly she ran to gather flowers to worship the sacred Lingam in the most devotional way.

When she returned an even more enthralling sight greeted her. The Lingam was situated on the banks of a pristine clear lake. While Parvati was walking back with flowers in both her hands, she saw one thousand cows, each one as white as jasmine flowers, come out of the lake. They marched towards the large Shivalingam in unison and began to pour all their milk over the sacred Lingam, bathing it with their liquid love. Once their udders had emptied all of the milk over the holy Linga, the cows went around the Lingam three times in circumambulation and then disappeared back into the lake.

Parvati was so fascinated by this incident that she decided to take the form of a cowherd girl and reside in that place worshipping the holy Shivalingam along with those celestial cows.

Those were happy days for Parvati. Though Lord Shiva wasn't there with her, she never felt his absence. The Lingam was a representation of her husband and serving the Lingam made her feel constantly connected to him.

One day things suddenly changed for Parvati. The peace and the serenity of the place unexpectedly evaporated. She felt some evil force lurking around. Someone with impure motives had entered that holy place. And the feeling was palpable to Parvati.

A shameless duo had entered into that city somehow. They were rakshasa brothers named Kritti and Vasa. When they saw the unparalleled beauty of Parvati, they were smitten with lust. With no qualms about the consequences, the two expressed their desire to unite with her. Just hearing these sickening demons speak such words appalled Parvati who disappeared from their sight. Venturing into a secluded place, Parvati prayed intensely to Shiva.

The very next moment, Lord Shiva appeared in the form of a cowherd boy and approached Parvati who was dressed as a cowherd girl. Recognising her husband, the great mystic Shiva, Parvati paid her respects. Understanding the situation, Shiva reassured Parvati that there was no need to be anxious about these tiny demons who have walked into their own death traps.

He narrated the history of these demons to Parvati. There was a king named Drumila who performed great many austerities and sacrifices to please the gods. Finally, pleased with his sincerity, the gods offered him a boon that he would have two sons who could never be killed by any weapon whatsoever it may be. Shiva ended the short story by saying that she would have to find a way to kill both of them without the use of any weapons. He smiled with confidence. He knew she would figure out a way. He blessed her that by the will of the Supreme Lord, she would carve out a path. As soon as he said that, he disappeared.

With a smile on her face, Parvati wandered around in the forest fearlessly. As expected, the two demons were hovering around her like honeybees hover around flowers.

This time instead of pushing them away, Parvati engaged in a discussion with them. She told them that she would fulfil their desire to marry her on one condition.

The two demons were thrilled beyond their imagination. They didn't even think this was possible. They quickly asked her to state her condition. Her condition surprised them. In fact, it made them giggle. Why would a delicate woman like her put up such a condition to extremely robust and powerful demons like them? Her condition was that she would become the wife of the one who could carry her on his shoulder. Carrying her would be like carrying a feather on their shoulders. They wouldn't even know if she was seated on their shoulders.

Initially they began to quarrel amongst themselves. Then later they decided that they would offer to carry her on their shoulders together. Surprisingly the beautiful girl agreed. The next moment, Parvati mounted on their shoulders and stood with one foot each steadily perched on each demon's shoulder.

The two brothers were beaming thinking about their fortune and the foolishness of the cowherd girl. But in a few seconds their smiles vanished. Their mouths began to contort in pain. Their faces were dishevelled in the agony they were experiencing. The once feather-light girl was now weighing like a mountain. She was becoming heavier by the second. Parvati had turned into Vishwambhari, the goddess of the world.

Who can bear the burden of the entire world on their shoulders? She crushed them under her weight and in a matter of seconds the two demons were buried deep into the earth. As soon as the two demons were buried in their graves, celestials showered flowers over her and declared her to be Bhubaneshwari, goddess of the three worlds.

But the result of Parvati assuming that form of Vishwambhari was that she became extremely thirsty. It was almost as if the thirst of the entire earth was assimilated in her being. Exactly at that point Lord Shiva appeared to join his wife.

Seeing his wife suffer such pangs of thirst, Lord Shiva struck a mountain with his trident and created a crater that instantly became a lake filled with fresh water. The lake created by Shiva came to be known as Shankar Vapi. But Bhubaneshwari desired to drink water from a reservoir that was properly formed with holy waters from all over the universe. Wanting to fulfil her desire, Shiva then instructed his bull carrier, Nandi to fetch water from all the holy places across the universe. Nandi fetched waters from Mandakini Ganga, and other holy places like Prayag, Pushkar, Naimisha, Prabhas, among many others.

When the waters arrived, Shiva created another crater close by and invited all the gods headed by Lord Janardhan and Lord Brahma to bless it. The second reservoir was named as Bindu Sarovar.

Once Bhubaneshwari drank water to her satisfaction, Lord Shiva invited all the gods to have bath in the two reservoirs. With great joy Shiva offered a blessing that anyone who bathes in the Shankar Vapi would attain the same qualities as him and anyone bathing in Bindu Sarovar would attain his abode.

Then Shiva requested Lord Janardhan to reside on the eastern side of the lake on his snake bed Anantashesha and take charge of this holy place. Since then, Lord Ananta Vasudev has been residing on the eastern bank of Bindu Sarovar and his remnants are offered to Lord Bhubaneshwar Shiva every day.

26

Here Comes Ganesha

It was a cool lazy afternoon at the scenic Mount Kailash. Perfect day to spend with loving friends. Parvati did just that with her closest aides, Jayaa and Vijayaa. It felt so relaxing doing nothing but idle chit-chat. Lord Shiva had gone out for the day and had left no hint about when he would return. Parvati felt very much at peace that day in the comfort of her friends' soothing chatter.

Their conversation took them all over the place, discussing subjects as mundane as their food preferences to as esoteric as Lord Shiva's erratic moods. Jayaa and Vijayaa, feeling at ease thanks to the cosy and warm atmosphere, ventured to make a few comments.

"Dear Parvati," said Jayaa, "all the ganas in Kailash are obedient to Lord Shiva. Although Nandi and Bhringin are more or less our own people, others cannot be called our own."

"I agree Jayaa," chipped in Vijayaa, "they obey only Lord Shiva and have no inclination to be in sync with our needs. Maybe it is time for us to create something we can call our own?"

Vijayaa was thinking aloud when she came up with the suggestion. Her own suggestion seemed rather intelligent to her and she beamed with pride.

Parvati was listening intently to her friends and somehow, everything they said made a lot of sense. She totally concurred with their practical ideas. It would be so nice to have someone who heard her needs and did what she desired. The ganas and *parsadas* were in a different world of their own, consumed by orders of their master.

She remembered times when she had asked Nandi to guard her room, only to be over ruled by Shiva who came in intruding her privacy while she was bathing. She had felt so embarrassed. Even thinking about it now made her turn beetroot-red. Had someone else been on guard, someone who was loyal to her, such occasions would cease to occur. That thought gave her a lot of satisfaction.

"Yes," she exclaimed, "both of you are so right. Imagine if we had someone to guard our privacy. Someone who took our commands without being side-tracked. Wouldn't it be amazing?"

Jayaa and Vijayaa nodded enthusiastically, glad that Parvati had latched on to their point of view.

Without wasting another moment, Parvati created a young boy from the dirt on her body. The boy was impressively huge which would enable him to protect her. He was handsome and brilliant, as well. After all, he belonged to her. She dressed him in rich clothes and ostentatious ornaments. She further blessed him with many benedictions. Finally, she said to him, "You are my son Ganesha. My very own son who will listen to me. I have no one else but you to call my own."

Ganesha said, "Mother, I will do as you say. What is it that you want me to do?"

"Dear son," said a pleased Parvati, "because you are my very own, I can be safe when you are guarding my apartment. Please make sure that no one enters without my permission."

Overwhelmed with love for him, she embraced him and kissed him. With a stick in his hand, he stood at the gate guarding his mother's privacy. Parvati, relieved to have someone who was her own to guard her, went to have a bath accompanied by her attendants and friends. She felt strangely light-hearted at her accomplishment. It had given her confidence a boost.

Outside stood Ganesha, ready to pounce on any visitor that dared to cross the threshold. He would smash him with his stick. He twirled his stick in attack mode, daring even a fly to pass through. As luck would have it, Lord Shiva, the master of Mount Kailash, appeared at Parvati's gate. Not knowing his identity, Ganesha waved his staff at him as if shooing him away. Never had anyone behaved like this with Shiva. Never ever!

"Where are you going? My mother is bathing. NO ONE can enter my mother's apartment without her permission." Ganesha even scolded him.

When an infuriated Shiva tried to ignore the insolent boy's words and action and made his way through the door, Ganesha struck him with his staff.

"You wicked boy," said Shiva, "Do you know who I am? I am the owner of this house. I am Shiva, Parvati's husband."

As much as Shiva tried to make Ganesha see sense, he just wouldn't budge. Ganesha had a single-pointed agenda, to guard his mother and he was adamant about doing that.

Shiva again tried to force his way inside and once again Ganesha struck him with his staff. Shiva backed off and standing outside, commanded his ganas to find out who the boy was and what he wanted. The ganas stomped inside and asked Ganesha defiantly, "Boy, what is your name? Why are you standing here blocking our way? If you value your life then please exit from here."

Ganesha retaliated, "Who are you and why do you insist on creating mischief here?"

The ganas laughed at Ganesha's ignorance. "We are Lord Shiva's disciples. Lord Shiva has instructed us to remove you from here so that he can enter his own house." They smirked, "We don't want to kill you because you look like one of us. So why don't you step aside and save yourself?"

If the ganas thought they could make Ganesha step aside with their soft words, they were in for a surprise. Fearless and undaunted, Ganesha stood his ground, glaring at them. If looks could kill, the ganas would be dead. Gauging that Ganesha had no intention of vacating his post, the ganas scurried back to Lord Shiva to inform him.

Lord Shiva erupted in anger, "Who does he think he is? Standing there and blocking our way! Surely, he wants to die today." He was equally put off with the ganas. "How is it that you are not able to eliminate him? Don't complain to me . . . just make sure you get rid of him.

The ganas went back to Ganesha to plead with him to let them enter. "Why do you stop us unnecessarily?" they tried to threaten him. "Do you not want to live?" they tried to enquire, "What do you want from us?" they used sarcasm, "How can a jackal be happy acting like a lion?" But nothing they said could move Ganesha from his duty.

When their taunts continued, Ganesha lost his cool. He struck them with his staff and said, "Go away before I do something worse and embarrass you."

The ganas did not know what to do. They did not really want to use violence. How could they create a scene at Mount Kailash? They were all servants of Shiva, including Ganesha and it was not right to fight amongst each other. Without retaliating, they returned to inform Lord Shiva.

Shiva, however, did not agree with them. Wielding his trishul in the air, he roared, "What is wrong with you? Can you not subdue a single boy? Go and beat him up if necessary. Enough is enough."

So chastised by him, the ganas went back. As this continued outside, Parvati heard the commotion inside. She sent her attendants to find out what was going on. The attendant came out and saw the argument between Ganesha and the ganas. She understood what was happening and went back mighty pleased to report to Parvati.

"Dear Parvati Devi, the ganas of Lord Shiva are here and they are having an argument with our own gana. Our gana is not allowing them inside and they are very upset. What I don't understand is how can they come anytime unannounced? Shouldn't they be following some etiquette? Let them fight it out and learn a lesson. Also, you will be happy to know that our gana is very impressive in not allowing them to enter. He's doing a wonderful job."

Parvati was pleased with her friend's input. So, she continued speaking, "Shiva always tries to take you for granted. But this time he can't. It's a big blow to his pride. Let us see what he does."

Parvati thought about Shiva. He was being too impatient to enter. Couldn't he wait a few minutes? Why was he creating a ruckus unnecessarily? She said, "Tell Ganesha to do what is necessary."

When Ganesha heard her message, he was relieved. Now he had full authority to stop the intruders. The message conveyed that he could use violence if needed. He thumped his thighs and arms and turned to the ganas, challenging them, "I am the gana of Parvati. You are ganas of Shiva. Let us see who wins now!"

Ganesha was openly challenging them to a battle. The Shivaganas wanted to be sure that it was alright to accept the challenge. So, they ran towards Shiva conveying to him that Parvati herself had instructed Ganesha to stop them from entering.

If the news alarmed Shiva, it did not show on his face. He said, "Although we don't like to engage in warfare, Ganesha has left us with no choice; imagine what people will say if they hear that Shiva got scared of Parvati and departed without fighting. It is demeaning for my reputation. So, hear me now. It is my wish that you accept his challenge. He is one and you are many. You will surely overpower him. So go and fight back."

Having clear orders, the ganas went to their camp and equipped themselves for the battle. Ganesha saw them coming, all ready for combat. He also geared up, "So finally you want a battle of one against many. Let Parvati see my strength now and Shiva yours. You have seen many battles in your life, but this is my first. And yet, if I defeat you today, how embarrassing it will be for Shiva!"

Grunting in anger and grinding their teeth, the Shivaganas ran towards Ganesha with full fury. While Nandi caught his left leg and pulled him, Bhringin caught and pulled the right one. Ganesha positioned his staff and smashed every gana that came close to him.

Some had broken arms and some broken backs. Some reeled with shattered heads and some crushed foreheads. Some had fractured legs and some had dislocated shoulders. Some fell on the ground and some escaped to inform Shiva. Like deer fleeing away from a lion, the ganas fled away from Ganesha. He was not a gana but lord Yama himself, causing widespread destruction at the end of a kalpa.

Now this terrible warfare attracted the attention of all demigods. They gathered at Kailash to enquire from Shiva if he needed their help. Shiva narrated the entire situation, how one boy guarding the door had created so much havoc. He asked Brahma to use his powers to deal with the boy.

Brahma left with the supreme confidence that a mere boy was no threat to him. As soon as he reached the heroic Ganesha, he plucked his beard and moustache. Anticipating a hit, Brahma said, "I am only a Brahmin coming to make peace with you. I will cause no harm."

Ganesha simply rotated his shining iron club to show his intentions. That was enough of a sign for Brahma to leave. Shiva then sent his army of ghosts and goblins along with Indra and his army to destroy the enemy boy. The huge numbers attacked Ganesha from every direction with all their might giving him no chance. The resulting tumult was so deafening that the entire universe was alarmed at the untimely destruction.

Parvati now got into action. She created two more of her energies to help her Ganesha fight. Both were equally powerful and fierce and together the three of them became a formidable force. None of the powerful weapons thrown at them had any impact on them. They were destroyed in a flash. It was indeed shocking how a single boy had stood firm and defeated practically the rest of the world. They were in fact scared of his club which continued to twirl in all ten directions threatening to kill them.

A battle like this had never been witnessed before. The earth quaked and mountains fell. The sky twirled and the ganas fled. Finally, the remaining ganas withdrew, with weapons all destroyed. They told Shiva that this gana was not an ordinary gana. There was something special about him. And if Shiva did not intervene, he would destroy the whole world. The surviving ganas begged Shiva to come and put an end to the boy's violent spree.

Shiva realised that nothing and nobody could match the powers of Parvati's gana. He seemed to be quite a superhero. None of the demigods could achieve anything against him. The king of heaven and the six-headed god, both had been rendered ineffective.

His blood boiling, Shiva walked towards the gory scene, unmindful of what he was doing. He soon found himself face to face with Ganesha. For Ganesha, it was do or die. Shiva himself was standing in front of him, determined to end his life. Ganesha mentally took blessings from his mother by touching her lotus-feet and gave Shiva a powerful blow with his staff.

Shiva's trident fell far away. Five of his arms were also injured. That was an amazing attack, thought Shiva, something impossible for his ganas to handle. Next, Shiva picked up his bow Pinaka and the trident. In a swift movement, he reached for Ganesha and cut off his head, using the trident.

With the falling of Ganesha's head, the universe came to a standstill. All activities stopped. Not even the air moved. Slowly the ganas came to their senses and started jumping madly with joy. Sounds of drums and bugles filled the air.

When news reached Parvati that her beloved Ganesha had been killed, she became as forceful as a forest fire. She resolved to create a universal deluge and drown all existence. Mad with rage, she created many more shaktis and ordered them to flood the world.

The shaktis got into action, destroying everything that came their way. Yakshas, rakshasas, demigods, celestials, everything was consumed by their fury. Not just the Gods but even Shiva was helpless in front of Parvati's wrath. When Parvati got angry, nothing could stop her. Everyone ran away from her.

Brahma, Shiva, and Vishnu got together to discuss ways and means to appease the goddess. They decided to send the peaceful sages to calm her down. The sages stood before her with folded palms and bowed down repeatedly. "O mother of the universe, O great goddess, please forgive those who sin. With folded palms we request you to give us our peace back."

With such calm and soothing words, the sages pacified the goddess till she reluctantly agreed to lower her fury. She said, "If you can arrange for my son to live again, I will stop the devastation. If not, I will destroy everything and you will never be happy."

The sages returned to inform the trio about Parvati's condition. Shiva agreed to do the needful to restore peace in the world. He directed the sages to go north, "Go north carrying the body with you and fit the head of the first being you meet.

The sages followed his instructions and started towards north. On the way they met a single-tusked elephant. They placed his head on Ganesha's body and carried him back. As Shiva glanced at the lifeless body, the sages sprinkled holy water and chanted mantras. By divine will, Ganesha became conscious as if waking up from deep sleep. Everyone rejoiced to see Ganesha awake. Parvati hugged her son and the universe was restored to normalcy once again.

27

Gopeshwar Mahadeva

He had never heard a sound so melodious in his entire life. It touched the very core of his heart and reverberated throughout his body causing an immensely soothing effect. Lord Shiva stood up immediately. He had to reach the source of that enrapturing sound right away. He could hear the melody emanating from a divine flute. If the sound was so amazing, how amazing would the person who created such a soul-searching music be!

Following the vibrations of the sound, Shiva found his way to the small village of Vrindavan. The sound of the flute seemed to be encompassing the entire village. It almost appeared to be a constant theme of the village. How fortunate must these villagers be that they got to hear this most divine sound day and night!

When Shiva entered the abode of Vrindavan, it was late in the night. The whole village was asleep. But the sound seemed to be coming from the outskirts of the village from the forest area.

Shiva, enthusiastic to reach the source of the sound, ran into the forest. He ran at a great speed till he reached a section of the forest that was brilliantly lit up. By the look of that place, Shiva immediately knew that something special was about to take place there. He had stumbled upon something that was undoubtedly a divine secret.

When he attempted to enter the flowery archway that seemed to mark the entry point into that lit-up arena, he was stopped. The gatekeeper was no ordinary one. She was Yoga Maya, the divine internal energy of the Supreme Lord. What he had stumbled upon was the Raas sthali, the divine abode of the supremely auspicious Raas dance of Krishna with the gopis of Vrindavan.

Yoga Maya explained that the rule of the Raas arena was that no male except Krishna could enter its precincts. Seeing his eagerness to explore the secret of the Raas sthali, Yoga Maya gave him an undisclosed tip. She said if he could turn into a gopi, then he could enter.

Now the obvious question was how could he possibly attain the form of a gopi? She had a solution for that too. Apparently, there have been some exceptions in the past and some format had been set for such exceptions. Shiva was eager to hear her suggestion.

Yoga Maya directed Shiva to Vrinda Devi who was the caretaker and manager of Vrindavan. Vrinda Devi personally orchestrated all the pastimes of Krishna in Vrindavan. She was an expert in creating unbelievably conducive settings in which Krishna could have the best of experiences.

When Shiva approached the goddess of Vrindavan forest, Vrinda Devi instructed Shiva to bathe in the pristine clear waters of the Mansarovar lake. Lord Shiva in his eagerness to participate in the supremely auspicious Raas dance of Lord Krishna, did exactly as he was told.

Lo and behold, from the lake emerged the most beautiful gopi in the universe. Vrinda devi was amazed by the transformation of Shiva into such a beautiful gopi. Guiding the new gopi, Vrinda devi brought her to the flowery archway where Yoga Maya stood. Seeing the transformation of Shiva, Yoga Maya smiled.

This time she didn't stop the entry. Shiva's heart was overwhelmed with divine love and gratitude for being allowed entry into the most confidential pastime of Sri Krishna. Every step into that divine arena of the Raas dance was special.

Vrinda Devi directed Shiva to one corner of the Raas dance arena. They were just in time for the beginning of the divine dance. Musical instruments of a hundred different varieties began playing in mystical rhythms creating an amazing symphony.

Once all the instruments were in sync and the tempo was set to perfection, the flute took the centre stage. Instantly Shiva's senses and mind experienced that very same thrill once again. This flute was instrumental in dragging him all the way from Kailash to taking the form of a gopi in the middle of the Raas dance arena.

Shiva absorbed every single bit of the divine flute emanating from the lips of Sri Krishna. There was nothing in the three worlds that was comparable to this bliss. Shiva noticed that all the musical instruments were totally in sync with the flute and did not suppress its sound. Then the coordinated dance began. Thousands of Gopis began to dance in such perfectly synchronised movements that it seemed that the whole earth was twirling joyfully.

Shiva joined in slowly, though he was dancing in a far-off corner, as he was new and untrained. But he caught up with the steps and found great joy in the divine devotional dance. Sri Krishna was right in the centre and just beside him danced the most beautiful of all the gopis, Radha. One single prayer emanated from the enraptured mind of Shiva at that point. "O Radha Krishna, O divine couple, please bestow on me devotion to your lotus feet."

When Shiva opened his eyes, he was shocked to be staring at the handsome face of Sri Krishna right in front of him. Krishna stood face to face before him smiling beautifully with his hand on Radha's shoulder. Sri Krishna said, "O' Gopeshwar, I am so happy to see you as a gopi. I bless you that all gopis for all time to come will offer their respects to you."

Hearing this, all but one gopi began to smile; only Radha frowned. She had never heard Krishna address anyone including her as Gopeshwar, which means the master of gopis. She demanded to know who this gopi was, suddenly getting all favours from Krishna. That's when Sri Krishna introduced Lord Shiva to the whole Raas Mandal and officially welcomed him to the Raas dance.

He then offered Lord Shiva the post of protector for the whole of Sri Vrindavan and he instructed all the gopis to offer worship to Gopeshwar Mahadeva every single day. To this day, Lord Shiva is protecting the holy land of Vrindavan in the form of Gopeshwar Mahadeva and he is worshipped by every single gopi ever since.

28

Shivratri

How did the celebration of Shivratri begin? From the Puranas and Shastras, we learn the story behind this spiritual festival that absolves one of all sins.

Bhilla was a cruel forest dweller who made a living by hunting down small innocent animals. He didn't care about them as long as his family was well fed. It was not just a means of livelihood for him, it was also his passion. He simply loved hunting. Addicted to the high of hitting his target. Felt nearly like God deciding which animal would die today and which animal would live. He was also ill-natured and short-tempered. As a result, he had accrued many sins in his lifetime.

It was an unusual day when in spite of hunting all day, he had nothing to show for it. No hunt meant his family would sleep hungry. This thought kept motivating him to go on. It was sunset yet he continued his search. Frustrated and hungry, he reached a cool placid lake. The peaceful water body gave him some hope. Like him, animals too would be coming here to drink water. Instead of roaming around the forest, he could station himself at the lake side and wait for them. Sooner or later, he would be rewarded.

With these happy thoughts, he looked around. The bael tree looked comforting and inviting. He scooped some water for himself and then headed towards the tree to perch himself on top of it. He would be safe with a clear view of the lake.

All he had to do was wait in his hiding place for an animal to come to quench its thirst. He made himself comfortable with one eye on the lake. Time was ticking and it was the first quarter of the night when he spotted a hind approaching the lake. Deer for dinner was a perfect meal, he thought.

As he moved to take aim, some water from his pouch and a few bael leaves from the tree fell down. Unknown to Bhilla, they landed on the Shivalingam below as an offering to Mahadeva from him. Mahadeva was pleased with the offering in the first quarter of the night which meant that Bhilla was absolved of a few of his sins.

The alert hind heard the rustling of leaves and turned around in the nick of time to see the hunter taking aim at him. Afraid to lose his life at that very moment, he called out to the hunter. "Why do you want to kill me, dear sir?"

Bhilla was taken aback to hear the hind speak to him like a human. Nevertheless, he replied back, "I need to feed my family. By hunting you down, there will be food on the table for my children and wife. I am only doing my duty."

The hind, instead of feeling sad, was happy to hear this. He said, "Dear sir, it is indeed a privilege to be of use to someone else. The merits gained by being useful for others cannot be achieved even in a hundred years. If my death can bring joy to your family, I am ready for it."

The hunter was too shocked to say anything.

"I have only one request," said the deer, "please allow me to drink water and go home once to say goodbye to my family. I have a husband, two children, and a sister too. They will wait endlessly for me, not knowing what has happened. Please sir, I promise you I will return to serve you."

The hunter knew now the hind was only trying to trick him into letting him go. He laughed at the deer's folly and said, "Do you think I'm stupid enough to let you go? Why will you come back? Of course, you won't!"

The hind said, "Do not think I am lying. The earth, the mountains, the river, all are founded on truth. Everything rests on truth itself."

But the hunter was unmoved. He wanted food for his family. The hind then said, "If I do not return, may I be afflicted by the sin of one who does not worship Lord Vishnu or Lord Shiva. Or the sin of someone who harms others. Or the sin of an ungrateful person."

The hind's pleas melted the cruel hunter's heart. He allowed the deer to go, extracting a promise that she would return. The hind pranced home feeling both joy and sorrow simultaneously.

The first part of the night had ended and the hunter had not slept at all. He had also been hungry all day.

Since the hind had not returned home, her sister set out in search for her. She too came near the lake to quench her thirst. The hunter, picked up his bow again. This time too, some water and bael leaves fell from the tree as an offering to the Shivalingam below. It was the second quarter of night and Shiva accepted the offering gladly, wiping away another portion of his sins.

The hind spotted the hunter and asked him his intentions. It was obvious of course, as the hunter once again expressed his need to kill the hind to feed his starving family. This time he was not surprised with the hind's answer. They all belonged to the same flock. The hind said, "It is indeed an honour to be of some use to others. I have no regret dying for a cause."

As the hind paused in pain, the hunter knew what was coming and he was not wrong.

"I have come to search for my sister. Can you please let me go back home so I can inform her and my family that I have this great opportunity to sacrifice my life for the benefit of another? I give you my word I will be back soon."

The hunter was in no mood to give in this time. He said, "Your sister was here and she told me the same thing, word for word. I, like a fool, let her go and she hasn't returned yet. Do you think I'm so foolish I will let you go as well?"

The hunter sneered mockingly and took aim.

The hind jumped up and down in panic. She had to somehow convince the hunter of her sincerity. She tried once again, "I am a truthful person and I shy away from sinning. If I don't return, it will be as much a sin as adultery, as much as forsaking the Vedic principles . . . believe me, I will not accrue these sins for anything in the world. I will come back for your sake."

The hunter, with a heart purified to an extent by now, could not refuse on compassionate grounds. He let her go. The happy hind galloped away to do the last chores of her life.

The second quarter of night had come to an end without the hunter having slept a wink. As the third quarter set in, he could barely control his glee when he saw a stout stag coming up to the lake. He swung into action taking aim and, in the process, some water and bael leaves were offered to the Shivalingam on his behalf. Lord Shiva gladly accepted the simple offering, erasing another bit of his sins. That's the benevolent nature of Shiva. Ashutosha Shiva. How easy it is to please him.

The stag sensing the hunter's movement, turned towards him.

"Pray, sir, what is it that you want to do? Kill me?"

The stag asked point blank.

"Yes, to feed my hungry children."

The stag felt a thrill run down to his tail. "It is my good fortune to use this body for your benefit. One must live for others."

The hunter had a deja-vu feeling. This was too much.

"I am certainly blessed that a well-nourished body like mine can be put to good use. But I have two children. Dear sir, I must give them a few words of consolation before I depart. I must ensure that they and their mother will manage after I leave."

The hunter, with a purified mind, replied gently, "Every deer that came this way has promised to return.

But none has. How can I believe you? How can I make a livelihood if I leave every animal? I do not want to believe your false promises."

The stag said solemnly, "Truth is the foundation of all existence. Lying will dissolve all my merits within no time. If I fail to return, I will be burdened by sinful reactions of not fasting on Shivratri or misappropriating another's wealth, or not helping another intentionally."

"You may go but return quickly," pronounced the hunter.

The stag quickly bounced back home to do the needful.

The two hinds, the stag and the two fawns were now together at the hermitage where they resided. Each one shared his or her experience. Since each one had individually given a promise, they were all duty bound to return and hand themselves over to the hunter. None wanted to accrue the sin of being a liar.

The senior hind tried to talk her sister and the stag out of it. "I was the first one to promise him so it shall be me who goes. How will our fawns stay without their father?" She wept at the thought of her fatherless fawns.

The younger hind said, "I want to go. Both of you can stay."

The stag said, "I will go, no more discussions. The children will be happier with their mothers."

Since none relented, they left the fawns with their neighbour and went to keep their promise with the hunter. The fawns, unhappy at being left behind, quietly followed them. They did not mind dying if the option was living without their family.

The loving group reached the lake and surrendered in front of the hunter. The jubilant hunter picked his bow again. And what happened? Without any realisation, he again offered water and some bael leaves to the Shivalinga. Once Shiva accepted his offerings, there were hardly any sinful reactions left for him. He had performed auspicious worship all through the night. Nor had he eaten all night.

The hinds and the stags said, "Sir, we are here to keep our promise. You may shoot us."

The hunter couldn't believe his eyes. The entire deer family was in front of him willing to sacrifice themselves. Each one wanted the other to live. Each one wanted to be of use for others. This triggered a chain of thoughts in the hunter's now purified mind.

These animals have more values than I do. They have no knowledge, yet they know of sacrifice. And I, a human being, have nothing to show in terms of a life based on goodness. I have tortured others. Harassed others. For my own needs and pleasures. Ever since birth, I have been sinful. How shameful!

Hanging his head in shame, streams of tears rushed down his face. He put his bow down, unable to complete the action. Somehow, words stumbled out of his mouth.

"Go home. I will not kill you."

He closed his eyes and broke down. Ashamed of his past life, he vowed to live now inspired by the morals from the innocent deer.

As soon as he whispered the words to the deer, something magical happened. Pleased by his transformation, Shiva materialised in front of him.

"You have pleased me," said the omnipotent Shiva, "by your all night fasting and offerings. Ask me any boon."

The hunter fell at Shiva's feet. "I am happy to see your form. My desire is fulfilled."

Shiva approved his humility and said, "From now on, your name is Guha. Your capital city will be Sringaverapura. You will flourish in every way. Even Sri Rama will visit your home. He will consider you as a loving brother. Serving him, you will attain liberation."

The hunter's transformation not only changed his future, it also liberated the deer family simply by getting darshan of Mahadeva. They left their material body for a divine body and a chariot took them to heavenly abodes.

Thus came the precedence of fasting all night on Shivratri to attain prosperity and salvation from the kind Lord Shiva.

29

Liberating a Ghost

For a woman, her husband is of utmost importance, even if dead! This was certainly true for Chanchala. Her husband had led such a sinful life that she worried about his afterlife. She worried where he would be and how he could be helped. The only way to help his soul advance higher was by divine intervention. Who else could help her other than mother Parvati?

She turned towards this embodiment of mercy with full faith that she would not be disappointed. It was Parvati who had lifted her out of her material existence after she surrendered her life to Lord Shiva. When Chanchala was on earth, she too had led a sinful life till her life turned around after hearing words of wisdom from a learned saint.

She happened to go to Gokarna to take a dip in the holy pond. It was there she heard that one could wash off all their sins by worshiping Lord Shiva.

From that day she felt so much remorse for her past actions that she decided to put an end to her sinful activities. The fear of Yama and the prospect of going to hell had motivated her to transform her life to one of simple devotion. The saint narrated stories from *Shiva Purana* to her and her heart had welled with detachment desiring liberation.

Blessed by the saint, she meditated on Shiva and this blissful existence went on for a long time. At the end of her life, with a fully purified heart, she boarded a divine aerial chariot which took her to Lord Shiva's abode.

There she actually saw the three-eyed lord with the brilliance of a million suns. He was ardently served by Nandi, Ganesha and others. She had bowed down to him again and again with great reverence. She was then gently ushered towards Parvati who captured her heart with a mesmerising smile. Parvati then engaged Chanchala as her attendant.

Recalling the mercy she had received, she approached mother Parvati with prayers and humility. With folded hands she said, "O' venerable mother, daughter of Himalaya, dear to Lord Shiva, Supreme Energy, please help me. You are the refuge of helpless souls like me. You are Knowledge, Existence, and Bliss."

Attracted towards her gentle demeanour, Parvati was pleased with Chanchala's devotion. She said, "I am always there for my devotees. Tell me what is it that your beautiful heart desires?"

Parvati's softness moved Chanchala to tears. She had lived an unhappy life bereft of any kindness. She broke into tears and confided in the goddess.

"My husband had deserted me for a prostitute woman. After he passed away, I do not know where he has gone because of his sinful acts. But wherever he is, I would like to help him. Dear mother, please take me where he is."

Parvati shuddered at the thought of what her husband had done. Even angry that her devotee had suffered because of him. Incensed at the injustice, she couldn't understand why Chanchala wanted to be with him or help him.

She easily saw where her husband was and said, "My child, your wicked husband Binduga was a sinful man. He was sent to hell to pay for his sins. After his quota of time in hell, he then went to Vindhya mountains and now lives there as a ghost. He suffered in hell and is suffering even now in the Vindhyas. He has nothing to eat but air and surrounded by all sort of miseries."

This terrible news numbed Chanchala even further. Her tender heart was unable to bear the pain of a loved one in misery. But Parvati's presence comforted her, giving her the courage to ask her for a solution.

"Pray tell me, what is it that can help free him of his sins so that he can attain liberation? There must be something I can do. I'm sure if you want, you can help him."

Parvati laughed. Chanchala was determined to do something for her wicked husband, come what may. She suggested, "If your husband can hear stories from *Shiva Purana* then he will surely be liberated."

"Do then arrange for an opportunity for him to hear Shiva Katha," begged Chanchala grabbing the opportunity to maximise on goddess Parvati's benevolence.

Parvati already felt sorry for her and seeing her determination, she agreed to arrange for that opportunity. King Tumburu was the perfect person for this task. She sent a message to Gandharva loka to intimate the Gandharva king Tumburu that he was needed by Parvati. Tumburu arrived immediately on receiving the message.

Parvati introduced Chanchala to Tumburu and advised the king, "Tumburu, you are just the man we need. You are a first-class expert in singing Shiva's glories and stories. Go with this good woman to Vindhyas. And narrate Shiva stories to her husband who lives as a ghost in those mountains."

Tumburu understood this was for the benefit of someone fortunate who Goddess Parvati wanted to favour. He looked at Chanchala and then at Parvati, waiting to know more about his mission.

"This is Chanchala," said Parvati, "her husband was a brahman who cheated her and left home for a prostitute. He never said his prayers and was immersed in anarthas. She is concerned about him and wants to help him get liberated. He is presently in the Vindhya mountains trapped as a ghost. I would like that you go there and narrate the *Shiva Purana* so that he can listen and get maximum benefit from it. Hearing the *Shiva Purana*, his sins will be wiped off and he will be freed from his ghostly existence. You will then bring him here in the aerial chariot to Lord Shiva's abode."

Tumburu was excited to carry out this wonderful service of bringing another soul to the ethereal world. Accompanied by Chanchala, he left in his chariot in search of the ghost in the Vindhyas. They found him there shouting aloud without any reason. He was huge with a crooked form. Using his noose, Tumburu caught hold of him. After that he made arrangements for a festival. Singing glories from the *Shiva Purana* was itself a festival.

Word spread that Tumburu was there, creating a mad rush among celestial sages to go and hear the auspicious *Shiva Purana* from him. Tumburu had bound the ghost who was compelled to sit there and hear too. Everyone present in that assembly felt awfully blessed simply hearing the seven Samhitas of *Shiva Purana* along with its Mahatmya. The divine sages felt totally content and went back to their respective abodes. The ghost Binduga too having heard the *Purana*, was freed from his sins and discarded his ghost hood.

Assuming a divine form, he climbed the chariot. The trio of Tumburu, Chanchala and Binduga returned to Kailash where Binduga was delighted to be in the august presence of Shiva and Parvati. Parvati accepted him as their attendant.

30

Neelakantha

Offense to a great soul is always detrimental to one's health, both mental and physical. The gods headed by Indra were doomed simply due to one mistake of Indra. They were literally reduced to poverty. They lost everything they had including their houses and posts.

Durvasa muni whom they had offended had cursed them to abject poverty and great misery. That's exactly what happened. Bali, the King of the rakshasas ransacked their kingdom and sent them all scampering. The miserable gods took shelter with Lord Vishnu who advised them to make a truce with the rakshasas and together churn the milky ocean tempting them with the possibility of obtaining celestial nectar of immortality.

Immortality was the only temptation that really worked on the Asuras easily and they fell for the bait. The churning of the milky ocean began immediately with Mandara mountain as the churning rod and Vasuki, the celestial serpent as the giant rope. The demons and demigods lined up on both sides of the mountain and began the churning process holding the body of Vasuki. Initially when the churning began, the Mandara mountain began to sink into the ocean bed due to its heavy weight and the softness of the ocean sand. When requested by the Gods, Lord

Vishnu appeared as a huge tortoise to hold the Mandara mountain on his back.

The churning continued and one of the first things that appeared from the milky ocean was a very dangerous type of dark poison called *Halahala*. The poison began to spread across the ocean and the whole milky ocean which was pure white began to quickly transform into a dark black liquid. The poison was so dangerous that all forms of aquatics began to die and the birds that were flying over the ocean were all falling dead by consuming the poisonous vapours emitting from the ocean waters.

When the Gods realised that they were unable to handle the power of the poison, they approached the Prajapatis who in turn realised that the only person who could help them deal with this emergency was Lord Shiva. They humbly approached Shiva to help deal with the crisis at hand and he graciously agreed. When Lord Shiva agreed to the proposal of the Gods, his wife was very much next to him. Even though the task was extremely risky, goddess Gauri did not even hesitate a little bit and she did not stop him for a moment. She in fact encouraged him to go ahead and serve the society through this selfless act.

Arriving at the venue of the churning of the milk ocean, Lord Shiva assessed the situation. By then the poison had disbursed across the entire ocean. The Gods and the Rakshasas stood far away from the effects of that poison and were watching helplessly as their venue was inaccessible to their churning business.

Lord Shiva closed his eyes and chanted the *Nama traya mantra*, while meditating on Lord Vishnu. As soon as he closed his eyes, the entire ocean experienced a tsunami like effect and all the poison which had by now accumulated on the surface of the ocean began to shoot up in the sky.

Shiva then held out his open palms to receive the poison. Holding the bottom end of the palm at his lips, Lord Shiva then waited for the poison to descend. The poison had formed an amalgam that rapidly descended like a fountain perfectly aimed at the palms of Lord Shiva. When the poison first hit his palms, it splashed and a portion of it landed on the floor at the feet of Lord Shiva. Many living creatures like snakes, scorpions' other insects and some types of plants hurriedly licked that fallen portion of the poison and thus became highly poisonous themselves.

Not allowing any more spillage, Lord Shiva began to drink the poison accumulating in the cup of his palms. Slowly the whole barrage of poison was absolutely within the control of Lord Shiva and had entered his mouth. But interestingly, all that poison did not enter his stomach. Goddess Gauri had sensed this danger of the poison entering the system of Lord Shiva and had cleverly caught the neck of Lord Shiva very tightly preventing the poison from travelling any lower than his neck.

Lord Shiva's neck was held upwards and he was fully focussed on not letting a single drop of poison fall anywhere else. The result of Gauri holding the neck of Lord Shiva in between was that the poison accumulated at the throat of Lord Shiva. So powerful was the poison that the entire neck of Lord Shiva turned bluish due to the accumulation of the poison in a circular band around his neck.

Rather than harming Shiva's body, the poison had become an ornament decorating his neck. From outside it looked like a necklace of blue cerulean shining effulgently. From then on, the gods named Lord Shiva as Neelakantha, the one who has a blue neck.

As soon as the poison was dissipated, the Gods and the Daityas rushed back to the churning once again. They had wasted enough time on this poison sorting. Now they just wanted to complete the churning affair and get their celestial nectar.

In the process of rushing back to assume their main agenda, they had completely forgotten to thank Lord Shiva and express their gratitude for his selfless contribution and sacrifice. Many days later one of them suddenly remembered that they had totally forgotten to thank Lord Shiva, their saviour.

Often one is so absorbed in one's own self-interest that matters of gratitude take a back seat and are mostly forgotten. Once the work is done, no one bothers to thank the one who helped. However, Lord Shiva wasn't looking for such appreciation and thanks. He did the task of drinking the poison as his service to society and to carry out the desire of Lord Vishnu. There was not an iota of self-interest in it. Thus, he did not take offense and immediately forgave those who sought his forgiveness.

In fact, to show the demigods that he had indeed forgiven them and was in a joyous mood, Lord Shiva began to dance. The day on which the Gods offered their gratitude to Lord Shiva was the *Trayodashi* day and the time that Lord Shiva performed his dance was between 4.30 p.m. and 6.00 p.m.

These one and half hours or two *muhurtas* are considered the time of *Sandhya Shiva Tandavam* or the dance period of Lord Shiva in the evening. In fact, that day Lord Shiva danced on the head of Nandi, his bull carrier. He tactfully and delicately danced in the small space between the horns of Nandi.

Great devotees of Lord Shiva believe that praying to Lord Shiva during this period of the day especially on the thirteenth day of every lunar month during the evening period is considered to get rid of all the sins of such a person. This ritual is famously known as *Pradosham*, which simply means the remover of *dosha* or faults. Just like Lord Shiva removed the faults during the churning of the milk ocean, similarly when one seeks his shelter, he will happily remove all faults from one's life.

31

A Close Shave

Narada had never expected to be stalled like that. Right in the middle of his journey, Vrikasura, the son of Shakuni, forcibly stopped him. He wanted an answer to his question immediately.

His question was—which of the three most powerful Gods, Brahma, Shiva, and Vishnu, was the easiest to please? Narada did not even have to think for a second. Pat came his reply. "Shiva! He is most easily pleased by exhibition of a little sincerity. If people like Ravana and Banasura could manage to please Lord Shiva, then anyone can."

Straightaway, Vrikasura proceeded to Kedarnath to engage in extreme levels of austerities with an aim to please Lord Shiva. Days passed and when Vrikasura saw that Lord Shiva wasn't appearing as quickly as he had expected, he began to shred off pieces of his own flesh offering them into the sacred fire. Part by part, he painfully continued offering portions of his body to the holy fire. Yet there was no sign of the appearance of the master of Kailash.

He finally decided to offer his own head as the final oblations into the fire. After dipping himself into the holy waters of the river, Vrikasura once again sat in front of the sacrificial fire and picked up a hatchet to chop off his own head. As he gripped the handle of the sharp tool to muster the strength to sever his head, his prayer was answered. Suddenly from within that sacrificial fire appeared the most magnanimous Lord Shiva. Quickly grabbing both the arms of the Rakshasa, Shiva stopped him from killing himself.

Vrikasura opened his eyes to see that his worshipable master had indeed appeared in front of him. Just with one touch of Shiva, all the wounds of his body healed and all the parts that had been lopped off appeared once again fresh and youthful.

Lord Shiva was smiling in the most compassionate manner. He could never handle the pain that entities heap upon themselves in order to please him. Of course, he never had such bizarre expectations from people who worshipped him. Just a little water offered with utmost sincerity was enough.

But somehow these Rakshasas always resorted to such extreme measures to prove their sincerity. He always wondered who gave them such thoughts and ideas of self-torture to win favours. Not sure about favours but these people definitely managed to gain attention immediately.

Wanting to put an end to the matter quickly, Lord Shiva asked Vrikasura what benediction he sought. The fervent nature of his desire shocked the soft-hearted Shiva. This strange man wanted the power to split someone's head into pieces by the mere touch of his hand. A boon like this was unheard of and extremely cruel in nature. But Shiva had already offered his word to him and thus, had to accede by granting it to him. Shiva knew that offering him such a boon was very much like offering milk to a poisonous snake. The natural result was that the poison in the fangs of the snake simply became more powerful, and the snake even deadlier.

As soon as Shiva pronounced his affirmation of the boon, the facial expression of Vrikasura changed and he began to step towards Lord Shiva with an ugly sadistic grin on his face. His hands were extended out and he was attempting to reach out to touch the head of Lord Shiva.

That's when Shiva understood his sinister intentions. Shiva panicked and backed off. The grin on the face of Vrikasura increased and he began to run towards Shiva, determined to touch his head as an experiment of his newly acquired powers. The first person he wanted to try it on was the one who offered him the boon in the first place. Words like gratitude didn't exist in the dictionary of Vrikasura and for that matter, in any of the asuras'.

Lord Shiva fled from his abode in the North and ran at great speed in any direction his feet took him. A hot pursuit followed with Vrikasura gaining ground. Shiva approached many of the great gods, but none could fathom undoing a benediction that the most powerful Lord Shiva had bestowed.

Shiva was trapped in the whirlpool of his own powers. And knowing this very well Vrikasura kept the chase on. Finally, the chase ended at *Shwetadwipa*, the earthly abode of Lord Vishnu.

Shiva knew that this was his last hope. Even before Lord Shiva reached him, Lord Vishnu realised the gravity of the problem at hand with Vrikasura chasing Shiva. Lord Vishnu decided to put a permanent end to this drama in an unorthodox way.

Waiting for the opportune moment, Lord Vishnu appeared in front of Vrikasura as a brahman wearing deerskin and carrying a water pot. He stopped the frantically running asura. The effulgent authoritarian look of the brahman made Vrikasura pause for a few moments to hear him out. The brahman began to make his inquiries. He called Vrikasura by his name and his father's name. That instantly caught his attention and he stopped.

The brahman said, "O' son of Shakuni, you seem to be very tired. It seems that you have been running a great distance. What desire do you wish to accomplish by venturing out so far? In order to accomplish anything big in life, it is important to take the help of those who are capable of helping us."

When Vrikasura heard the sweet voice of the gentle brahman, he suddenly felt like trusting him with his problem. He had already been chasing Shiva for quite some time and had yet been unable to catch up on him. Vrikasura poured out his heart and shared all his plans with the brahman.

Hearing this, the brahman started laughing loudly. Vrikasura wasn't able to comprehend the reason behind that sudden laughter. The brahman explained to the confused Vrikasura that Shiva could never be trusted. Someone who has been cursed so badly by his father-in-law Daksha, can never be trusted to give boons that were effective. In fact, the brahman continued to state that of late, Shiva had been offering many boons to various people and the boons have all been ineffective. Thus, his credibility was diminishing slowly.

Vrikasura was very confused now. His strategy completely depended on the fact that Shiva was powerful and his boons never went in vain. But now the element of trust was lost. What was he to do now? The brahman nonchalantly said that Vrikasura could just sneak his fingers over his own head to see if any part of his scalp burnt, to verify the efficacy of the boon of Lord Shiva. If nothing happened, then he would be sure that Shiva had lied to him.

Now, Vrikasura somehow saw some logic in that suggestion. The very next moment Vrikasura's head ruptured into smithereens and that was the end of the tormentor.

The moment the asura was dead, victory cries originated from all directions and the celestials showered flower petals. Lord Vishnu assumed his original form and spoke to Lord Shiva who had joined him by then. With great tenderness, he explained to Shiva that this person is destroyed as a result of his own sins. Of all the sins Vrikasura had committed, Lord Vishnu explained, the greatest one was that of offending Lord Shiva, the spiritual master of the universe.

32

Amarnath Cave Secret

Nestled in the cold peaks of the Himalayas at a height of 12,700 feet, is the very significant Amarnath Cave. Pilgrims sometime spot a pair of pigeons flying around and they are believed to be eternal. Their immortality and the Amarnath Cave are intricately connected.

Shiva had chosen this cave at a height nearly impossible for anyone to traverse for a very special mission.

One day Lord Shiva found Parvati sulking, not even looking him in the eye. When he asked her the reason, she disclosed with tears welling her eyes, "Why is it that you are immortal and I am not? Unlike you, I have to take birth again and again. Isn't that unfair?"

Shiva wiped her tears and said, "It is due to the *Amar Katha*. I know the secret to immortality." As he said this, he fell silent. He dared not say more. But Parvati caught on and insisted that he tell her the Amar Katha. After a lot of persuasion from Parvati, Shiva agreed to tell her the story of immortality.

But he could not tell the secret in open air. At Kailash, they were not alone. Anyone could drop in and listen to the secret saga. What they needed was a place so secluded that no one would know where they were. Only then he could be sure that no one was eavesdropping. Mentally, he searched for such a place and finally settled on the Amarnath Cave, high up in the Himalayas, far away from normal habitats.

They left their abode at Mount Kailash and reached Pahalgam in Kashmir. Since the real journey to the caves by Shiva and Parvati started from here, pilgrims believe they should walk from Pahalgam when on Amarnath yatra.

To be doubly sure, Shiva instructed his loyal servant Nandi to stay guard and make sure that they were not being followed—to ensure he had all the privacy he needed. Not a single creature was allowed to trespass. This place is thus known as Bailgaon. He then left a series of spies to watch out after them.

A little distance ahead, Shiva dropped the moon, at a place now known as Chandanwadi. At Lake Sheshnag, Vasuki kept vigil. At Mahaguna Parvat, it was little Ganesha. And finally, the Pancha Mahabhootas were positioned at Panchtarini.

Even with so much vigilance, Shiva was still not satisfied. Arriving at the Amarnath Cave, he created a Rudra named Kalagni. Kalagni lit a fire around the cave to discourage anyone from going further.

Satisfied with the elaborate precautions, Shiva held Parvati's hand and led her inside the cave. Once inside, he laid down his deer skin asana and sat in Padma yoga. After a brief meditation, he began narrating the Amar Katha to Parvati at an auspicious *muhurat*. The *Mrityu Rahasya* and *Amar Rahasya* were the secrets of immortality which he shared with Parvati in confidence.

In this cave, Lord Shiva manifested as an ice lingam which waxes and wanes with the movement of the moon.

On the full moon day of *Shravan* (*Raksha bandhan* day), the lingam attains a maximum height of six feet. Gradually, it wanes and fades out on new moon day. There are two more ice lingams in the cave, of Parvati and Ganesha.

And what about the pair of pigeons? In spite of all the precautions Shiva took, he missed the presence of two eggs in the cave in which he spread his deer skin. Two pigeons emerged from the eggs and heard the entire narration of Amar Katha verbatim from Shiva. The fortunate pigeons attained immortal status and can still be seen by the pilgrims on their way to the Amarnath Cave.